LIFE ON SARK

D1440387

Cover:
Above: Scene at the Water Carnival;
Below: The Seigneurie in winter.

Overleaf: Map of Sark

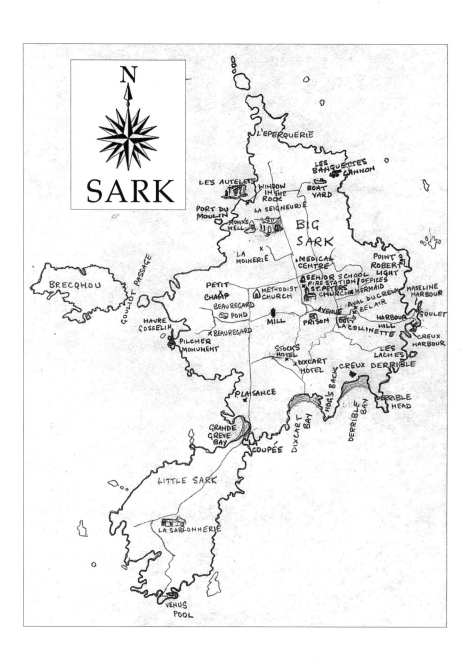

LIFE *on* SARK

Through the year with
Jennifer Cochrane

SEAFLOWER BOOKS

Published in 1994
New edition 1996 by
SEAFLOWER BOOKS
16$^{1/2}$ New St. John's Road
St. Helier
Jersey

Seaflower Books is an imprint of
EX LIBRIS PRESS
1 The Shambles
Bradford on Avon
Wiltshire
BA15 1JS

Typeset in 10 point Palatino

Design and typesetting by Ex Libris Press
Cover printed by Shires Press, Trowbridge, Wiltshire
Printed and bound in Britain by
Cromwell Press Ltd., Broughton Gifford, Wiltshire

ISBN 0 948578 63 7

THE MASELINE QUAY AT HIGH TIDE

APRIL

IT MAY SEEM STRANGE, STARTING an account of life on Sark in April. In other places, a year starts in January and runs to December. Sark life, however, is ruled by considerations other than the calendar. The weather and the seasons play a large part in shaping the island activities. We are starting at April because that is when the Sark season usually begins. Sark's visitors arrive in force from Easter until the autumnal gales disrupt the boat schedules at the equinox, and so we'll begin our look at life on Sark with the visitors, at Easter.

~

The first impression of the island is of somewhere completely different. To begin with, the only way to get to Sark is by boat. Planes are not allowed to fly over Sark under 2000 feet, let alone land here. The island's parliament occasionally gives permission for a helicopter to land or to fly over the land, and sometimes gives permission to light aircraft to overfly to take photographs, and planes are allowed to land in an emergency, but these flights are usually years apart. Visitors come by boat.

The daily boats start running between Guernsey and Sark on the Monday before Good Friday. Most of the hotels open in time to receive resident visitors who want to spend Easter on Sark, and for the first time in the year Sark residents can pop over to Guernsey on any week day.

April is a good time to make a dental appointment! After the rush of Easter, the visitor numbers drop again to give the residents both time and available boats, so children get their new shoes and any other shopping that requires a personal appearance in Guernsey can be done.

The next surprise for visitors is the unmetalled roads. To people who live in an asphalt world – roads and pavements underfoot, houses blocking the views and the green confined to gardens and parks – the sight of gold-coloured dusty lanes between high banks covered in flowers comes as a pleasant change. The first introduction to the harbour hill can be unsettling, but old Sark hands welcome the walk up the sun-dappled surface, beneath the arching trees.

The path on the left hand side of the road tempts a lot of the visitors to enjoy a closer look at the wild flowers and to reach the plateau, high above sea level, at a leisurely pace, but there is a ride up the hill. Two tractor-drawn harbour hill transports, affectionately known as the toast-racks, meet the boats and carry those who don't wish to walk up to the top. They can't go any further. Sark law forbids the transport of people by tractors. A tractor driver may have one person with him to help with a job, but otherwise passengers are left at the top of the harbour hill where they can walk, hire bikes or have a trip in a horse-drawn carriage.

Sark itself looks absolutely beautiful in April. It's bluebell time. The shady ground under the trees on either side of the harbour hill turns a misty azure, and the damp morning air carries the faint scent of the flowers, a delicate, hyacinth-like perfume. The blooms on the côtils, the steep fields above the cliffs, appear earlier than those in the woods, staining them blue and making a trip round Sark by boat a feast of beauty.

The season is heralded by a traditional event. For a very long time, certainly well before the memories of the oldest inhabitants, Sark children – and some of the adults – have gathered at Beauregard Pond on Good Friday morning to sail model boats. The age of the boats gives some idea of how long this custom has been practised. One of the boats is about 150 years old, and two more are very near their centuries.

Sailing model boats on Beauregard Pond on Good Friday morning.

The weather is sometimes unpleasant; there have been years when it was difficult to see the other side of the pond, as the mist clamped down. Some years have been very cold, but that doesn't stop eager youngsters from wading thigh-deep to free their sailing boats from branches overhanging the water. There are modern remote-controlled speedboats joining the sailing boats today. Come to that, there are do-it-yourself models made from polystyrene, plastic and toothpicks which sail very well. It doesn't matter what it's made of, the important thing is to be there, with some kind of vessel.

Sark won't let a fundraising opportunity like that get away. There is a stall selling hot cross buns (cold!) and hot coffee or chocolate by the pond nowadays. The cause varies. It may be the RNLI, which plays an important part in the life of the island, or the Red Cross, or some other such institution, but someone, somewhere, will benefit from the comforting hot drinks!

By that time, the larger boats are back in the water. Sark doesn't have a really safe harbour, so the fishing boats are put ashore for the winter. There is a closed season for shellfish, too; it is illegal to put out a lobster pot between the end of October and the first of April. So there is great preparation and the mobile crane drops the boats back into the water ready to start catching crabs and lobsters in April. The first shellfish of the year taste delicious!

The horses come out of their winter rest to stand patiently at La Collinette waiting for their daily passengers, although their drivers are still mostly local this early in the year. As the first of the summer drivers arrive, they sort out the harness, stored for the winter, and clean it, and the carriages, and get everything ready for work.

On the Saturday, the flower ladies spend a long day decorating St Peter's Church for Easter Sunday. Every window-sill, the pulpit and the choir stalls has its floral covering, and the altar, lectern, organ and font, every lamp standard and bookcase has a flowery decoration. The scent of the blossoms greets both locals and visitors who call in to see the church *en fête*.

Easter Sunday fills the church, the choir having prepared a special anthem and practised hard to make a splendid sound. The island is not unduly religious, but the two churches, St Peter's and the Methodist Church, each has a loyal congregation and often join together for an ecumenical service. The Methodist Church usually has a lay preacher, so any christenings, weddings or funerals take place in the parish church, which has an ordained priest.

The parish church is firmly linked with island life. At one time the island's official notices were read out in the church, so that everyone would hear them or hear of them. Eventually the church objected to this and now official notices are posted in a box on the church wall, beside the door. Later a second box was put up at the top of the harbour hill, at La Collinette. Most people pass by there fairly frequently, so that there is a good chance that official notices will be read in one of the two boxes.

~

The Easter meeting of Sark's parliament, called Chief Pleas, takes place on the first Wednesday after Easter. Sark, like the other Channel Islands, is not part of the United Kingdom. It is an independent state, making its own laws and managing its own money. It is the smallest independent state in the Commonwealth, and the last feudal state in the western world. Part of the Bailiwick of Guernsey, it is not governed from the larger island, but shares with it the Queen's representative, the Lieutenant Governor, and the Royal Court. Guernsey laws have no power in Sark unless they are ratified by Chief Pleas, which sits three times a year, with extraordinary meetings if they are needed. Guernsey taxes do not apply in Sark; the island levies its own taxes, which do not include income tax.

Chief Pleas sits in the Senior School. Teaching is not disrupted for the Easter meeting, because the children are on holiday. The Seneschal presides at the meeting, sitting in a beautifully carved wooden chair which has a protective box over it during schooltime. The Seigneur sits next to him in another carved chair, and the officers of the court and the Constable and Vingtenier take their seats on the dais for the meeting.

The house is made up from *tenants* and deputies. The *tenants* are the people who hold the leases of the forty *tenements* on the island. When Helier de Carteret settled on Sark in 1565, he was granted the fief by Queen Elizabeth I on condition that he kept Sark inhabited and had forty men with muskets ready at all times to defend the island. Helier de Carteret, the first Seigneur of Sark, divided the island into forty farms, called *tenements* and brought families from Jersey, where he was Seigneur of St Ouen, and from Guernsey to live on the farms. The forty *tenements* still exist today, and the lease-owners, called *tenants*, still take a seat in Chief Pleas.

There were only landowners in Chief Pleas until this century, when Sark's laws were changed to allow the non-landowners a voice in the government of the island. Deputies of the people were first elected in 1922 and elections are now held every three years. Chief Pleas meets three times a year, at Christmas, Easter and Michaelmas, the Easter meeting usually taking place in April.

~

After Easter and Chief Pleas, Sark settles down into the season's routines. There are often competition finals still to be completed after a winter of heats, quarter-finals and semi-finals in darts, quizzes, euchre, shove ha'penny, cribbage, pool and billiards. Each pub has its own competition, and some take place in the Island Hall, so the finals stretch over into the season, into the quiet time after Easter and before Whitsun.

Other celebrations take place in April; it is the month usually chosen to launch any boats built on Sark over the winter. Sark's boatbuilder was trained by his father, whose boats are still in use about the Channel Islands. The demand for boats is not large enough to allow a full-time occupation for a boatbuilder; the boatbuilder builds houses and runs a charter service to earn his living. The boats are built over the winter in spare time by a small but loyal team.

April is the best month for launching. The pressure of summer work has not developed, the weather is usually reasonably calm, the island is still fairly quiet. Launching a boat is a great occasion. First, the boat comes out of the boatshed. Because Sark is bounded by dramatic cliffs, there is no room at the harbours for a boatyard. Indeed, there are only three places where boats can get down to sea level. The first landing to be used on Sark, the Eperquerie landing, is still in existence, with a rough track descending to it, but it would be difficult for a trailer to negotiate today. The harbour hill is the only roadway to the sea, connecting the plateau with the old harbour, the Creux, and the new harbour, the Maseline.

The new harbour is the commercial harbour, and by April there are two ferry sailings a day from Guernsey, with four on Wednesdays and Saturdays and several boats from Jersey. With the cargo trips, the Maseline Harbour is in constant use.

The old harbour is the one used by local fishermen and boatowners and by visiting yachts. It is usually free of commercial traffic, sheltered and picturesque, and it is the ideal place for a launching party in April.

The first problem is to get the boat from the boatyard, 250 feet up to the north, down to the old harbour. The transfer was made by manpower when the boatbuilder's father was working, the boat on its trailer pulled along the narrow lanes by a team of men. Today, the tractors make moving boats a much easier task, and make the building of larger boats possible. The size limit is set by the width of the tunnels through to the harbours. Both harbours are approached by tunnels blasted through rock curtains, and a boat has to be able to pass through them.

Manpower is still needed to move the boat out of the boatshed on to the yard, where the mobile crane can lift it on to the trailer. This is an evening task, but the journey to the sea has to start early in the morning, before the horses are on the roads. Horses do not take kindly to unusual, large road traffic: even small containers upset some of them!

The boats always take the same route. The tight Z-bends by La Tour, on the north-east coast, block the most direct path seawards. The procession of tractor, trailer, crane and bicycles passes across the north of the island, squeezes round the heart on the north-west corner and moves steadily down the Seigneurie road. It turns the Clos à Jaon corner quite easily, and goes down the Rue du Sermon to the Carrefour.

Once upon a time, there was a gate across the north end of the Rue Lucas – the stone gate-hinge still projects from the side of the

Carrefour cottage into the roadway. It makes the road less than 15 feet wide, and needs to be negotiated with care. If a boat can get through the tunnel, it can get past the gate-hinge, however, so the Carrefour is passed with some caution.

There is no other problem until the sharp bend at the top of the harbour hill, by the Power Station. That overcome, the descent to sea level is no problem today. In the past, the men had to hang on to ropes at the back of the boat to stop it careering away down the hill, which is one in four in places! With tractors and a crane, slowing the boat's progress is easy.

You can't build boats over a certain size on Sark – they must be able to get through the tunnels leading down to the harbours. Here the Non Pareil is cautiously backed through the Maseline tunnel by boat-builder Lawrence Roberts just before her christening and launch on Easter Monday, 1982.

The final stage, getting through the tunnel, is nerve-wracking even with a fairly narrow boat, but, with time and plenty of guidance, it is accomplished and the new boat finally comes to rest on the Creux quay, ready for the launch.

Launching is usually on another day, when ballast and other adjustments to the new boat are completed. A food-laden table, a celebration cake and plenty of beer and wine await the well-wishers who gather on the quay. The boat is blessed by the parish priest, the champagne crashes against the prow to give the vessel a name and the mobile crane swings the boat into the water with the owner aboard. A maiden voyage, trips for the guests and another Sark-built boat begins its life.

Launching another L.O. Roberts boat, the Genesis, later in the year.

The last of the winter activities over, the island turns its face to the season. Each part of the season has its own batch of visitors. Many who come in the spring for the flowers book again for the spring next year, so we are used to seeing April faces or May faces and each month sees the return of its old friends.

By the end of April, the season is well established and the quiet winter months are part of a distant world. The bluebells vanish under a canopy of unfurling ferns and red campion stipples the banks and fields, with buttercups and daisies. Thrift and sea campion decorate the cliffs, decking the island in flowers to welcome May.

~

La Collinette

MAY

Maytime, playtime,
God has given us Maytime
Thank Him for His gift of love;
Sing a song of spring.

THAT WAS A SCHOOL HYMN from a half century or so ago, which re-surfaces every year as the days lengthen and the bird song increases to deafening proportions. Sark is quiet between Easter and the Spring Bank Holiday, the weather is good, and there is some time to play.

Strictly speaking, it isn't spring in Sark, it's early summer. The bare-branched trees grow a fresh, green canopy to mask the distant shining of the sea while the sun shines straight along the lanes in the morning and the evening to blind cyclists. The hotels all open for the season and the population swells as the hotel workers and the carriage drivers arrive for work. Some are returning, but others have responded to advertisments in the trade papers; they don't know Sark at all.

Horses and carriages with driver and carriage-owner together on the front seat circle the island as newcomers are trained and young Sark men pay extra attention at disco evenings in the Mermaid as the waitresses and chambermaids investigate island entertainment while there is still spare time.

~

Although the celebrations have diminished with time, May is remembered as the month the island was liberated after the war. Sark's Liberation Day was 10th May 1945. The day is burned into the memories of those who were on Sark that May. News of the surrender of Germany filtered through to islanders from the illegal crystal sets late on Monday May 7th. Curfew-breaking Philip Perrée heard the news with Mr and Mrs Hubert Lanyon, and went home to La Tour to rouse his father. Charlie Perrée was Constable at the time and really should have arrested his son for curfew-breaking, but was convinced that the news was true and there would be no curfew on Tuesday 8th. The pair of them erected the flagpole which had been hidden since 1940 to fly the Union Jack. Then Philip was off again, to Stocks Hotel, to wake Bertie Falle and decorate the yard with flags, ready for the morning wakening of the German soldiers living in the hotel.

On Tuesday 8th, Sibyl Hathaway ran up the Union Jack and the Stars and Stripes, in honour of her American-born husband, who was in prison camp in Germany. She also invited all the islanders to the Island Hall at 3pm to listen to Prime Minister Winston Churchill's broadcast, in which he said "our dear Channel Islands will be liberated today". The islanders could see HMS Beagle anchored in the Guernsey roads, but they didn't hear from anyone. They waited and watched, and then decided to celebrate anyway. They built a giant bonfire near the Pilcher Monument, the only victory bonfire in the Channel Islands on the day the war ended.

There was a dance in the Island Hall that night, with mass curfew breaking, everyone dancing away to the music of a two-man band. Silence fell as a German soldier walked into the Hall – but he had come with cigarettes, a present from the troops to the revellers.

Wednesday was a long, anxious day, with still no word from the liberating troops or from the German soldiers. These were all still fully armed, and no one knew what they would do. Had they been instructed to resist to the end? Would they obey orders if instructed to fight? The German soldiers locked themselves in the Manoir, their headquarters, and would not communicate. As the only telephone on the island was in German headquarters, and the soldiers would not answer it, the other islands did not know what was happening on Sark, either. They had seen the huge bonfire near the Gouliot headland, but did not know who lit it. Was it Germans, causing trouble? They had no way of knowing that it was celebrating islanders.

As Wednesday progressed and no word came to Sark, bewilderment and depression spread. Uncertainty grew and people went to bed in quite a different mood from the elation of Tuesday.

Thursday May 10th dawned with no more news, but in the afternoon Brigadier Snow managed to release a small force of 12 men under Colonel Allen to cross from Guernsey to Sark in a Naval tug. Watchers on Sark saw the boat coming, and the Dame went down to the Creux Harbour to welcome the British Army.

The news went round Sark like wildfire, and people dropped what they were doing and rushed to the top of the harbour hill to greet their liberators. The soldiers marched along the Avenue, throwing cigarettes and sweets to the ecstatic islanders, to Le Manoir. They were accompanied by a German officer, sent to take over the command of the troops if the commanders caused any trouble. They didn't. The Naval officer handed his dirk over as a symbol of surrender – the dirk was returned to Sark by the officer who received it in May 1985, the fortieth anniversary of the Liberation.

The Dame, who had acted as an interpreter for the surrender, was left in charge of the three hundred German soldiers, as Brigadier Snow needed all his small body of men on the other islands. For the first time for five years Sark was free!

For many years Liberation Day was celebrated with a cavalcade, with fancy dress parades and dances, but slowly the custom died.

The decades are still celebrated, but the annual holidays have gone as Sark decided that the war was over and it was time to think of other things. The holiday air has stayed, however, and Sark still has a regular visit from the In-Pensioners of the Royal Hospital, Chelsea, round about Liberation Day.

The Chelsea Pensioners are always welcomed to the island, taken on a carriage ride, given lunch, and a drink and they meet the Sark schoolchildren. The schools have built up a strong link with Chelsea Hospital over the years. Many of the children write to the inmates and the In-Pensioners invited the children to their mess for lunch on a school trip to London in April 1985. The Queen Mother invited the school party into Clarence House gardens for a chat on the same trip.

~

May is the month for Royal visits to Sark. The Queen Mother invited the school-children after her visit to Sark in 1984. She also visited in May 1975. The Duchess of Kent came in 1985, the Queen and Prince Philip in 1989, Princess Alexandra in 1990, the Duchess of Gloucester in 1992 – all in May.

Most Royal visitors arrive by air. That in itself is exciting. Bright red Wessex helicopters of the Queen's Flight, with an Army or Navy helicopter in attendance, do a trial run, landing in either the Cattle Show field or the school playing field. Horses are kept near the field to accustom them to the unexpected noise; in fact, Sark must be the only place where a helicopter is met by a wagonette!

The school-children are usually invited to look at the aircraft while the Queen's Aide and Guernsey's Lieutenant Governor go over the programme with the Seigneur, the Seneschal and the Constable. The Army or Navy back-up liaise with Sark's volunteer Fire Brigade to ensure that safety measures will be sufficient in an emergency and the final preparations are discussed.

The Royal visitors arrive about a week after this, to be met by the Seigneur and Mrs Beaumont, the Seneschal and all three schools, all 36 or so of them. The Queen Mother, a keen gardener, always contrives to spend time in the Seigneurie gardens and usually spends quite a bit of time with the children. The Duchess of Kent came to celebrate the fortieth anniversary of Liberation. Princess Alexandra saw an exhibition of occupation food and memorabilia – and involuntarily shared her posy with Appleby, the horse between the shafts of the victoria in which she was riding! The Duchess of Gloucester opened the new fire and ambulance station and island committee rooms. She was fascinated by the tractor drawn ambulance and fire tanks and spent a lot of time chatting to the fire crew. Like all the Royal visitors, she was charming; there are no anti-monarchists on Sark. We often meet members of the Royal family and find them all hard working and very good with people.

A trial run for the Wessex of the Queen's Flight, landing in the Cattle Show field before a Royal visit. The Seigneur and the Lieutenant Governor are in the wagonette.

Her Majesty and Prince Philip do not arrive by helicopter. They come in the Royal yacht Britannia and come ashore at the Maseline quay by Royal Barge. The Maseline Harbour was actually opened by Prince Philip, accompanied by Princess Elizabeth, in 1949 – in June, not May.

The Lieutenant Governor and his wife, the Seigneur and Mrs Beaumont, their heir, Christopher Beaumont and his wife and the

Constable and Vingtenier meet the Queen on the quay. There the Queen touches the short wooden batons carried by the Constable and Vingtenier, offered to her to assure her of their service.

When the Queen visited in 1978 as part of her Silver Jubilee tour, Seigneur Michael Beaumont swore allegiance to her. He knelt before her in the Island Hall – it was drizzling and the ceremony moved indoors from the Horse Show field – put his hands between hers and, in French, swore to be her liege man and to defend Sark in her name. His grandmother, the Dame, had done the same in 1957, setting a precedent. It was the first time that a Dame had sworn allegiance to a Queen; Sark usually has a Seigneur.

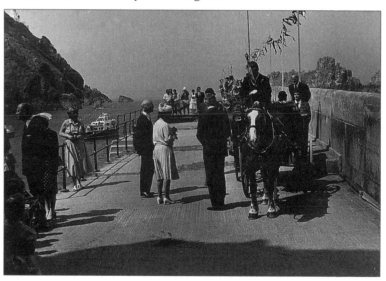

Horses and carriages line up along Sark's small quay, waiting for Her Majesty Queen Elizabeth, who has a good look at the victoria while Prince Philip talks to children.

In 1989, Her Majesty opened the new Medical Centre, and met Sark's older residents in the Island Hall. She walked from the Centre to the Hall, with the crowds following her along the sunny road and not a barrier in sight. Good manners ensured that the Queen was not crowded; Sark is probably the last place in Britain to work on that principle. Certainly there is nowhere else that she can ride peacefully along flowery lanes with just a sprinkling of people about her. Sark is closed for Royal visits – any stranger would be recognised instantly as such in this small community. Special Constables are sworn in for the occasion, but the whole island provides a guard!

~

May attracts other visitors to Sark, the combination of good weather and not too many people making it ideal for filming. It must be one of the most filmed places around. Television companies from all over the world come to record life without the motor car, feudal life at work, life in a small community – dozens of other projects. They all end up enchanted by the beauty, cameramen going into raptures over light, views, old buildings and the generally picturesque environment. Small films are often made here, with the odd full length one. The last major production was four hourly episodes of 'Mr Pye' for Channel 4 Television.

Mr Pye was written by Mervyn Peake, who lived on Sark while he was writing his famous Gormenghast trilogy. He set *Mr Pye* on Sark and the Landseer Film Company decided to film on the island when they found that most of the places mentioned in the book were still here. The stars were Patricia Hayes, Judy Parfitt, Derek Jacobi and Richard O'Callaghan. Sark residents got some speaking parts, Kevin Adams as a carriage driver and Tom Long as a schoolboy. We were very amused when the whole thing was screened. Kevin is Sark born and bred, but they decided he didn't sound Sark, and dubbed his lines with a dreadful accent, never heard in any of the Channel Islands; certainly not here!

We all had a marvellous time being extras. We all learnt a lot about film-making, got used to getting dressed up, going in to make-up, getting to the site for the day's filming, being given first positions, second positions, third positions, and hearing the assistant director saying 'Back to first positions' time and again. We stood in the sun in the cattle show scene – filmed in a field near La Jaspellerie, which became Miss Dredger's house – and watched one of today's best act-ors at short range. Our faces burnt in the hot May sun as the scene was shot again, and again, and.... We ran along the stony Port du Moulin beach enveloped in evil smelling smoke blowing in from a foam rubber whale. We were all drenched as we sat with plates of food in the picnic scene – a cloud appeared from nowhere and produced a very local downpour, so that we all had to go back the next day and do it all again.

The end result was great fun for us, we spent our time people-spotting. The series sold well, too, and for a couple of years we had visitors from all over the world coming to Sark because they had seen the series and liked the look of the island. The actual story was very strange, but very close to Mervyn Peake's book, which is also very strange.

A car in the Avenue! Man-powered! Filming 'Mr Pye' in 1985. The car was a camera platform, its engine disconnected.

Mervyn Peake had first visited Sark in the 1930s. He helped to found the Sark Artists group, which displayed their works in art galleries in London. Sark's present post office is in the Gallery Stores, named because it was built as an art gallery by the Sark Artists in the '30s. Mervyn Peake returned to Sark with his family after the

Derek Jacobi plays Mr. Pye in the TV series. Director Michael Darlow (left) tells the Sark extras what he wants them to do.

Second World War, in which he was a war artist. He was very distressed by the sights he recorded in Belsen. He was one of the first group to enter the camp. Mervyn Peake took refuge in Sark's tranquility to help him get over the experience, but contracted Parkinson's disease and returned to England for treatment. Signs of Sark's influence can be seen in the twisted plants drawn in Gormenghast and Mr Pye illustrations – they are taken from the wind-twisted branches of Sark's trees and shrubs. Mervyn Peake's daughter Claire returned to Sark during the filming of Mr Pye and had a part in the final, fly-ing scene.

~

This peaceful interim period, with just a morning and an afternoon boat from Guernsey on most days, ends with the spring Bank Holiday at the end of the month. Daily boats from Jersey have been increasing as the weather improves and the Guernsey ferries switch to the high season pattern to make life busier. Carriage tours are more frequent, there are more cycles on the roads and fewer vacancies in hotels and guest houses.

The Music Society concerts enter into the summer pattern. We do have live performers out of the high season, but it is much easier for busy artists to get to Sark, and leave again in time for their next performance when there are plenty of boats. Even with six scheduled boats a day there can be problems, however. If the wind comes up the boats may be disrupted, and there have been occasions when prestigious artists have been marooned on Sark, waiting anxiously for the wind to die down and let them continue their tour. We are grateful for a chance to hear musicians, singers and sometimes actors as an audience – but it's still more fun, being a film extra!

~

LA COUPÉE

JUNE

THIS IS THE MONTH OF long, sunny, blue and gold days and of dark blue and silver nights. The summer nights are a revelation to town dwellers. Sark has no street lighting and widely spaced houses. There is very little light from the ground at night; nothing to dim the glory of the stars. They spread across the sky in the great arc of the Milky Way, bright enough to see by. The constellations stand out clearly from the myriad twinkles, the Plough and Casseopeia slowly circling the North star as the night passes, the planets brilliant in the evening and morning sky.

Moonlit nights are not so good for stargazers, but make the use of torches unnecessary. The landscape is bathed in cold, white light, the shadows stark black across the roads and tracks. Out to sea, there is a silver path across the blue-black water, Guernsey, Herm, Jethou and Brecqhou outlined darkly against the shimmer. It makes walking home after an evening out a real pleasure.

The mornings begin early, with a melodious alarm call from the birds. Venturing out on to the dewy grass, the air still chill enough to make the nostrils tingle, the adventurous meet a barrage of song. Blackbirds fluting their territorial call from the branches; starlings, the brilliant mimics, stealing sounds from sparrows, chaffinches, robins, thrushes as well as telephones and bicycle bells; the spine-thrilling cries of the herring gulls; the wheep-wheep-wheeep of the oyster catchers echoing inland from the sea and, loveliest of all, the descending curtain of trills from the sky-lark high overhead, invisible against the clear sky.

Fishermen put to sea in the daylight, whatever the tide, and chug through a duck-egg blue sea shining round dark rocks. From the shore the wakes of the boats curl dark from their sterns across a smooth surface. They spend a long day pulling in lobster pots, taking out the crabs and lobsters and throwing back the small ones or those in berry, the boats followed by eager gulls, snatching the old bait from the surface waters for their breakfasts.

Fishermen at work – the float on a string of lobster pots goes over the side.

As the sun rises higher, the farmers are out and about milking the cows, checking on sheep and goats, feeding the hens and looking at the hay. Haymaking is still a co-operative effort, although the advent of the great circular bales has stopped the friendly collecting and stacking of bales which made hay gathering a working holiday in the past. It is not so long ago that the corn was bound into sheaves and stooked and schoolchildren were paid sixpence to count the sheaves and throw every tenth one on to the dîme cart for the Dame. The dîme cart is still on view in the Seigneurie grounds. Many of the farmers make silage rather than hay now, but the early stages of cutting and turning can still be seen – and smelt – round the island. This is one of the few places left where you can have genuine hay-fever!

The carriage drivers walk to the fields to collect their horses, take them back to the stables and groom them, to be ready for a day's work. The carriages are cleaned, the harnesses given a quick rub and off they go, horse and driver, to meet the incoming morning boats and the day's visitors. June is a quiet month despite the number of daily boats, and the drivers have time to chat to their passengers without the urgency of the high season.

Some of this atmosphere is captured on film. Occasionally the May shooting schedules extend to June, and one of TV's best known policemen spent a few days hunting criminals without his famous sports car. In 1987 Bergerac crossed from Jersey, chasing villain Ronald Pickup. John Nettles and the rest of the Bergerac crew staged a hair-raising fight on La Coupée, Ronald Pickup nearly pushing John Nettles off one of the rock outcrops half way across the precipitous isthmus. Since cycling across this eight-foot-wide link between Big Sark and Little Sark is forbidden because of the danger, and passengers in carriages have to dismount and walk across to get back into their vehicles on the far side, fighting there is not to be recommended, except for stunt men. La Coupée has had its fair share of tragedies; locals treat it with great respect, particularly in wild weather.

The resident visitors set off on their walks or rides, renewing their

Filming 'Bergerac' in 1987. Above: John Nettles outside the Post Office.
Below: Bergerac races along the quay at Creux Harbour after villain Ronald
Pickup, who was escaped to Sark.

knowledge of favourite bays. The cliff tops give wide views, and a chance to look down on the backs of the gulls, swooping from cliff to cliff or sitting on eggs in the isolated areas. Shag fly low across the waves, a couple of hundred feet below, looking for shoals of fish, and the lone fishermen in their small boats follow suit, hoping to run into the favourite summer fish – mackerel. Fresh mackerel, bought from a local fisherman, straight from the sea, grilled with mustard butter and served with new potatoes and young peas – one of the tastes of summer!

The long, light evenings are enjoyed by locals and visitors alike. Both take advantage of the open hotels and walk or take a carriage out to one of them for a meal. Sark residents keep a close eye on the new chefs, and don't hesitate to say if a meal is good, or if it is bad. Part of the island's reputation for good food comes from the honest opinions of the locals, who will report any backsliding.

Sark does have good chefs on the whole; the British Epicure Society often has holidays on Sark, because the general standard is so high, and the availablity of fresh fish and shellfish and home-grown vegetables is boosted by a good supply of veal stock. Sark has Guernsey cattle, as it is part of the Bailiwick of Guernsey, and only really good bull calves are kept for breeding. The rest are snapped up by the hotels for the table! At least those eating veal on Sark know that the calf led a normal life before its slaughter – no one here pens them up and feeds them hormones; they have been out to grass for much of their short lives.

Guernsey cattle have another advantage; they produce rich, golden milk, so rich that many people ask for skimmed. The resulting cream can be found in the shops, hotels and tea gardens, and in the home-made ice-cream on sale about the village. The ice-cream maker, Mary Nicolle, won a national Young Farmers competition with her traditional ice-cream. The natural flavour takes a bit of getting used to. We tend to think of vanilla ice-cream as plain ice-cream, but of course, it isn't. You can't have plain ice-cream flavour with most commercial ices, because they are not made from real cream. Mary's is, and the flavour of natural ice-cream takes a lot of beating, once you have banished vanilla from the memory.

~

One of the high spots of the year for Sark's older residents takes place in June. On an island without motor transport, getting round the island can be difficult as you grow older. Horse and carriage rides are very much a special treat for islanders, and are not a usual manner of travelling. For those with arthritis, or some other disabling disease, walking far is out of the question, and so many of Sark's older residents very rarely get to see friends at the other end of the island, or to see new buildings. So the Skilled Driving Society revived an old custom, and arranged a Midsummer Drive for older residents.

A sight familiar to Sark inhabitants, but different and exciting to visitors – the horses and carriages setting off to tour the island. This is the start of the Midsummer Drive in June.

At first the drive took place on Midsummer's Day itself, the 24th, in the evening, after work, and there was a dinner in the Island Hall, following the drive, at which people had a chance to sit and talk to one another. There would be songs and games and it would go on until the small hours of the morning. Various residents would invite the drive to drop in for a drink on the route of the drive. That was fine in warm weather, but then there were a spate of chilly or foggy Midsummer evenings and the drives got shorter and shorter to stop the guests from being chilled. We were losing the point of the exercise! Then Chief Pleas granted the Skilled Driving Society permission to have carriages on the road for six Sundays a year to allow competitions to take place on a Sunday. Normally horses and carriages and tractors must be off the road on a Sunday. Tractors doing essential agricultural work may be used, and a horse and carriage may take passengers to church, but no other four wheeled transport is allowed. The Sark Skilled Driving Society held competitions on a Saturday until the numbers of passengers coming to the island on a Saturday and wanting carriage rides made the competitions very difficult. Sunday competitions were the answer, and Chief Pleas agreed to a limited number of Sundays.

The committee then thought that perhaps an afternoon drive would be more enjoyable to its guests than an evening one. The Constable, when asked, gave permission for one of the competition Sundays to be used for the Midsummer Drive, and that is how the very popular Sunday Midsummer Drive came about. The passengers are invited by the Driving Society to join the drive, the main aim being to take those older residents who rarely get a chance to see Sark round their island. More mobile residents who are friends are also invited to the party, as are the doctor and the clergy to give them a chance to meet people who they would only see otherwise in a professional capacity.

Age alone is not a qualification for the drive, which often confuses newcomers to the island, who are used to a welfare state with benefits for old age pensioners. Sark does not have old age pensioners. It is not a welfare state, and people live in their old age on the money they have saved through their lives. The island will help those in financial difficulties, but not as a right. People who receive help from the island are 'on the parish' according to older Sark residents, and there are those who will not accept any help. They still think they should be able to manage their lives themselves, and accepting help is giving in.

They will accept an invitation to take part in the Midsummer Drive, and look forward to it. Someone offers hospitality to the Drive every year, and the halt for drinks is kept secret, as is the destination for tea. At the beginning of June committee members are engaged in guileless conversations full of inviting suggestions as to where the drive could go this year, but all in vain. So far drinks and tea have always been a surprise!

~

The other major June event comes towards the end of the month. Like any country community, Sark has its exhibitions, and the Midsummer Show is the time for the gardeners to display their skills. There are two competitions, the gardens themselves and their produce. The garden categories are 'Cottage gardens' and 'Gardens visible from the road'. All through June the gardeners are out weeding, dead-heading, tidying and worrying. Will there be a strong wind or a storm on the day before the judging? Will there be a sudden attack of black spot, leaf mould or aphids too late to deal with? What else could go wrong? It is amazing how often a sudden summer storm arrives on the Monday, with the show on the Wednesday. Still, everyone is affected together, the gales don't usually pick on just one garden!

Getting exibits to the show is an art in itself. Entries are accepted on the Tuesday evening or early on Wednesday morning. Some exhibits are easy. The popular home-made wines and sloe gin categories will not deteriorate overnight, nor will the children's handicrafts. But what of cut flowers and flower arrangements? Will the Island Hall get too warm overnight so that the flowers blow? Can one risk it? Some do, some get up at 5 am and collect their exhibits. Some flower arrangers take everything to the Hall and arrange there, some do them at home and carefully walk to the Hall, praying that no gust of wind will alter the position of the flowers and leaves. The children have to do their arrangements at the Hall under supervision, just to make sure that it is all their own work!

The children design and make miniature gardens for this show and create miniature flower arrangements in unusual containers. Thimbles, tiny ornaments and shells are regular entries, along with a variety of inspired originalities. Children's classes run from under seven years to twelve and over; even children who go to boarding schools in Guernsey or Britain take part if they are on Sark at the time of the Midsummer Show. Taking part in island events is bred into the younger members of the community by the Sark families; incomers do not always see that having a go is part of what makes Sark such a pleasant place in which to live, one of the strands of community life.

The adults enter roses and a variety of summer flowers, along with soft fruits and hors d'oeuvres. Flower arrangements include an arrangement of wild-flowers, which are short-lived, so that the arrangers may be met wandering through the woods and fields on Tuesday, searching for the blooms they have decided upon. They can be seen standing as if in a trance when they have chanced upon some particularly beautiful hedge flowers, and are rapidly re-adjusting their ideas – they may even be muttering to themselves. Visitors are not to be alarmed! It's only a symptom of pre-exhibitionism! It doesn't last.

Sark's island shows are very well staged. The main hall is en-circled by tiered tables covered in gleaming white cloths, with another row down the centre. The standard green vases hold glowing blooms which scent the air, with an undersmell of clean linen and a blast of soft fruits as you walk through the door. Is there anything more mouthwatering than the perfume of fresh strawberries? On the dais the silver and crystal cups sparkle in the afternoon sunlight, the whole room being the perfect encapsulation of civilised summer living. The judges come to Sark from Guernsey, to make quite sure that judging is free from local entanglements. It is not easy to be impartial in such a small community! The cups and prizes are presented at the end of the afternoon, when the children are free to accept their rewards.

~

Towards the end of the month life begins to take on more of a high season flavour. The French holiday season is approaching, and the number of day visitors from France via Jersey increases. The working day gets longer and more hectic and the number of bicycles wobbling about on the roads is greater. Both British and French visitors who have not ridden a cycle for years decide to see the island from wheel level. The drawback for the locals is that the British all ride on the left – as we do – but the French believe that our proximity to France means that the right hand side is the legal side. So one is liable to round a corner to find bicycles clean across the road, all convinced that they are not breaking the law! Whoops!

~

VENUS POOL AND L'ETAC

JULY

JULY, AND THE NUMBER OF visitors increases and the sea begins to warm up. The high season is in sight and the Sark schools' end-of-term activities mark the completion of another school year. Some of the children will leave the island for their education after this month. Sark provides an excellent education, but it is too small an island to afford laboratories or specialist teachers, and children cannot take national examinations from Sark. Those who want to go on to a higher education have to go to Guernsey or to Britain.

~

Education on Sark is free and the island is obliged by law to take children into its three schools. The island was a pioneer in education; it was made free and obligatory in 1827, when the Boys School was built. Today the ratio of teachers to pupils is amazing to mainlanders. It is about 1:11 normally. Teachers coming to Sark from elsewhere find the children a dream to teach. They are interested and, growing up in such a friendly, secure environment in which they know almost everyone, they will happily converse with adults and ask questions.

Official visitors frequently comment on their unselfconciousness.

Even model schoolchildren look forward to the summer holidays, however, and the announcment that the Mile Race will take place starts the run-up to the end of term. The whole school has a go at the Mile Race, and there are cups for infants, juniors and seniors. The distance is measured out on the island roads, and it is run early on a Friday morning, before the horses and carriages can cause complications.

In a school in which the ages of the children are spread out, it is inevitable that the older, larger children will win the races. There are not enough children in any one age group to provide peer-group competition, so that what the children learn is that you cannot always win, but it is fun to take part. They also learn that sooner or later, as you grow older, you will end up among the winners in all the sports! Taking part is demonstrated as the thing to do, which probably explains the enthusiasm brought to almost every project by local residents. They will always have a go!

Inside Sark's Senior School. The classroom is used as the House of Parliament by Chief Pleas.

In the past, before the term ended, the children had a holiday, on a Wednesday fairly early in the month, for the Sark Cattle Show. This annual event contributed to the high standard of the island's pedigree Guernsey cattle. The quality of the cattle was illustrated by the last Show, in 1992, when Sark played host to the World Guernsey Cattle Federation delegates, in Guernsey for their 7th Conference. They were impressed by the standards maintained in such a small island.

As in other islands in the Bailiwick, only Guernsey cattle may be kept on Sark. They are kept disease-free, and any imported from other islands undergo stringent tests before they can come ashore. Horses, too, are tested to make sure that they don't bring in anything nasty. In the past all Sark's milk supply was untreated, with no pasteurisation to spoil the flavour. Part of it still is today, so the cows must be guaranteed free of tuberculosis and similar diseases to be allowed to supply the milk.

The Cattle Show was heralded by days of cattle grooming, making sure that the placid animals look their best. Guernseys are gentle creatures on the whole. Even the bulls are good-natured on the Seigneurie farm. They are brought up pegged in the paddock near the gardens, where they see plenty of visitors. From calves, they are used to being patted and stroked, and they grow up liking people. The great bulls are approachable, and enjoy a back scratch, but it is as well to remember that even the best of them have bad days, and not to get too close if they are being irritated by heat or flies.

The Cattle Show used to be at Dos d'Ane, moved to the Bel Air field, then went to the Mermaid field and then to La Longue Pièce, still called the Cattle Show field, for many years before moving to the Horse Show field, adjacent to La Seigneurie. The Cattle Show field was large, but had no trees to provide shade in hot weather. The cattle stood in patient lines in the hot sun while the judges from Guernsey assessed their points. The Horse Show field is surrounded by trees and was a far more attractive site for the show, having plenty of shade all through the day.

The Lieutenant Governor of Guernsey usually visited the show to present the prizes, and members of the Royal Family have done so on past occasions. The two most sought after cups, for the best cow and the best bull, were a gift from the Queen. So the Cattle Show was an important event in the island calendar and the children enjoyed grooming their particular calf or cow and leading them round the roped enclosure under the eye of the judges. The Cattle Show ended because the pattern of cattle-keeping changed. From most households having some cattle, with three or four larger herds on the island, the cows became concentrated into fewer, larger herds, so that the farmers were virtually competing against themselves in the Show. So in 1994 the Committee decided to suspend the Show, the cups went into storage and the children lost a day's holiday!

Children had a day's holiday for the Cattle Show in July.

~

After the Mile Race on Friday comes the Swimming Gala, usually on the following Tuesday, although that depends on the weather. Hotel Petit Champ has allowed the children to learn to swim in their solar heated pool for many years and that is where the Swimming Gala is held. It is not a very long pool, and the emphasis is not on speed swimming, but on distance and life-saving techniques, both useful if you live on an island.

The schools' swimming sports make a very pleasant afternoon out. The lawn overlooking the pool is sheltered, there are friends sitting about and the children's efforts are very entertaining. The older children are each assigned to one of the very young, who will jump from the poolside into the arms of their senior with great confidence. The seniors are always around in the water in case they are needed, and the youngsters with arm bands and floating pads will cheerfully tackle a width, knowing that help is very near. They quickly become confident enough to swim, and their parents are then much happier when they are on the beach or out in a boat.

The School Sports Day follows the swimming sports, and that is held in the School Field at Clos à Jaon. The competition suffers from a wide age range here, too, but there are still running races, egg and spoon, skipping, hoops, wheelbarrow – all the traditional races of a summery day. The parents' race varies from year to year, but always causes much amusement among the children. It isn't until something like a race that you realise how old your children think that you are. Inside you feel that with a bit of hard training you could compete with the most famous, while outside the children see you as a doddery old soul who can just about walk up the harbour hill!

There is an Open Day in all three schools before the end of the year, a chance to see what they are all doing, to admire paintings, drawings, projects and books. Everyone is welcome, not just parents; the whole island is interested in the children and the schools. La Société Serquiaise visited the senior school for one of its meetings, and members seized the chance to investigate the computers which are everyday equipment in schools today, and a closed book to many of the older members of the community. They threw themselves into playing computer games for the first time and enjoyed using the educational programs. It is easier to keep in touch with the younger generation on such a small island!

The prizes are presented in a small ceremony, and that is the end of the school year. Many of the children have summer jobs, but families do make time to get down to the sea, down to the old harbour, where the children can swim easily, or along the gentle downward slope through Dixcart woods to Dixcart Bay. If it is possible to take a whole day, the tide is right and the family is the right age, then the precipitous path to Derrible may be negotiated, or the steep hairpin bends down to Grande Grève.

Both these beaches are like something out of an adventure story. Rupert Bear could easily appear on Derrible with his pals, exploring the echoing cave open to the sky through the Creux Derrible, searching the rock pools for animal life or playing in the sea, warm as it runs in across hot sands. Laying on one's back and watching the seabirds glide from cliff to cliff on the up-draughts could easily lull a body into a trance, but the need to keep an eye on the tide and to get across to the rocks at the bottom of the steps before the sea cuts them off from the beach stops too much daydreaming.

~

One of the July events which also stops daydreaming is the Sark to Jersey Rowing Race. This involves Jersey and Guernsey rather more than Sark, but local crews do compete, and occasionally win cups. It takes place on a mid-month Saturday, and starts from just off Dixcart Bay. The bay is crowded with working boats, fours, pairs, singles and dozens of escort boats. Each competing boat has its own escort in case of accident. There is always a crowd of accompanying on-lookers as well. The view from the path to the Jaspellerie across to the Hog's Back reveals nothing but boats, with the odd twinkle of water between.

The Seigneur of Sark usually starts the race with a small cannon from a large yacht. The rowing boats line up in a great arc, stretching between two marker boats, their escorts behind them, under the steep cliffs of the Hog's Back. On a clear day we can see Jersey miles away on the other side of waves, currents and unidentified hazards, although sometimes the starting gun goes and the boats break out of the long curve to vanish into a wall of grey mist. It's an inspiring sight on a fine day. The blades glitter as they plunge in and out of the sea and the light merges with the bright sea, the slender racing shells just shadows in the blaze of brilliant white. The fast fours get to Jersey in about two hours, but the heavy work boats may still be rowing four hours later. Sark is very proud of its entrants; they do finish, however long it takes them.

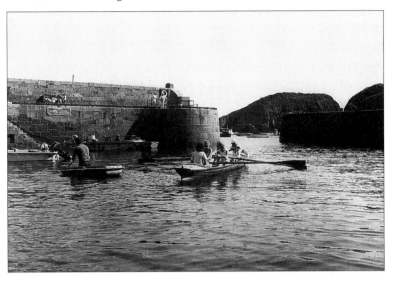

The Sark Ladies' coxed four prepares for the Sark to Jersey Rowing Race.

Periodically July is enlivened by an island christening. It is a good month, as family and friends can get to Sark easily and the work is not as intense as it will be in August. The christening is a family affair, but the whole congregation of St Peter's Church takes part. Christenings are usually incorporated into a Sunday morning service; visitors are delighted to be able to take part in a part of island life. The service is not the traditional one, from the Book of Common Prayer, but a blend of ancient and modern which involves the congregation in welcoming the child into the church.

No Sark dweller passes up an excuse for a party, and what better excuse than a christening. Parents, godparents and guests repair to Mell's in the Avenue, or more rarely to a hotel, to wet the baby's head, and they are often still there when folk are making their way to their hotels for dinner. There are usually a few who find it difficult to concentrate at work on Monday!

In a dry month the volunteer fire brigade keep their ears open for an alarm calling them to the dreaded cliff fires. These are usually caught in good time, but we still remember 1976, when the cliffs at Plaisance, above La Coupée, burned for three days. Water was very short, after two dry summers and a dry winter, but tankful after tankful was pumped over the gorse to limit the fire. It was ironic that just fifty feet down the cliff was a plentiful supply, But that was salt and even if the brigade had possessed pumps powerful enough to raise sea-water, the equipment would have been damaged. The fire was contained, the men who had worked in relays for three days with very little sleep collapsed into bed and today all traces of the great patch of scorched earth and blackened branches are buried by fresh grass and shrubs.

~

July 1983 was when Sark took delivery of its first mobile crane. This was not an easy arrival. The crane could not be unloaded on to the Maseline quay because the wooden jetty was not strong enough to take its weight. The piles would have to be strengthened with steel girders to take the strain, but the girders could not be positioned without a mobile crane. Impasse! The army came to the rescue, but it took time. The crane sat on the Cambridge berth in St Peter Port harbour for nearly two months while the ramp-powered lighter from 17 Port Regiment, 51 Squadron of the Royal Corps of Transport underwent a refit. The Royal Corps of Transport offered its help because landing a crane on Sark made an interesting training excercise.

The lighter *Medway* crossed the Channel from Southampton and the 15-ton crane was loaded aboard by Guernsey's 20-ton crane and the laden lighter crossed to Sark to arrive in the Creux harbour two hours before high water. The 72 foot-long boat was manoeuvred into the tiny harbour and crossed it to the small shingle beach under the cliffs. After two attempts the ramp was positioned and Sark's first crane driver, Mr Peter Elmont, went aboard and climbed into the cab of the crane and drove it on to the pre-prepared tracks on the beach.

~

The lightened boat was able to up ramp and back off, leaving the crane perched on the edge of the sea.

At that stage the end of the slipway up to the quay was underwater. There was a long wait in the sun watching the tide turn and the water retreat from the back of the vehicle. Another track was laid in a curve to the end of the slipway and when the tide had gone down enough, the crane was turned on the slipping shingle and it crawled across to the granite slipway, the planks being moved from the back to in front as it moved across the beach. Success! It reached the end of the slipway safely and crawled up to the quay, carefully negotiating the curve round the cliff. Everyone heaved a sigh of relief when it was on level ground.

The new mobile crane waits in the Creux Harbour beach for the tide to go down and uncover the slip.

The next hazard was the long tunnel, but that proved to be no problem. The new crane then drove through the Maseline tunnel on to the quay, before returning to its parking area alongside the Island Store between the harbours. Its first job was to strengthen the piles of the Maseline jetty so that the crane could move on to it if necessary.

Sark has not looked back since that July. The crane is invaluable, and it is difficult now to remember how we managed without it!

~

Sometimes, if the tide dictates it, Sark has its Water Carnival in July. Guernsey's Round Table always has a July Carnival, and in 1984, Sark decided to add their mite to the Guernsey celebrations. The year before, Lawrence Roberts had converted an old whaler into a Viking longboat, and, suitably attired in Viking helmets and somewhat smelly garments made from old hippy coats, goatskin rugs and anything else that looked appropriate, they took their round shields and long swords, climbed into *Igor* and set off across the sea. They swept into St Peter Port harbour mouth under sail and, roaring a Viking yell, descended upon the delighted crowds, wrested several pretty bank employees from their job of counting money, flung them over their shoulders, made for the boat and put out to sea – well out of the harbour, anyway!

The girls were kept prisoners for all of half-an-hour, and released when their employers paid ransom to the Round Table. Rape and pillage did well for the Guernsey charities that July!

~

THE SEIGNEURIE FROM THE GARDENS

AUGUST

AUGUST, THE HIGH SEASON, THE hectic month when there are not enough hours in the day or days in the week. The harbours are full of ferries from Guernsey, expeditions from Jersey and visiting yachts from France and England. Fishermen pop in to greet Sark friends, little boats from all the other islands bustle in and out of the harbours. Up on the top of the island the roads are thick with bicycles and the carriage seats are almost all full as the horses set off on their island tours.

The carriages plod along the dusty roads, disturbing clouds of butterflies fluttering round the horse droppings in the road. They rise in colourful flurries from the roadside flowers. Sark does not use pesticides and is rewarded with a treasure trove of insects and wild flowers. A Royal Botanical Society expedition found 600 species of wild flowers on Sark one summer. Bees drone among the blossoms, but the wasps and biting flies are not appreciated by anyone, particularly the horses and their drivers.

~

It may be a busy month, but that doesn't stop the fund-raising. The first August event is the Traditional Fair arranged by St Peter's Church. It was started in 1979, when we discovered that the church needed extensive repairs that we could not afford. That first fair raised £1,100 and it has been going strong ever since. We bought and paid for roof repairs, bell repairs, an organ and general redecorating. We manage to pay the ever increasing quota to the diocese and generally keep the church functioning.

Advertising the Church Fair at La Collinette.

The fair is set up in the Vicarage garden in the evening of the first Friday in the month. A loyal group of helpers appears every year to set up a loudspeaker system, to hang the bunting – improved by new strings bought for the Queen's last visit – and to unload and assemble the tents and tables. On Saturday morning the crabs and lobsters, home-made cakes and jams, local cream and butter, items for tombola and bottle stalls, white elephant material and all the traditional church fête goods arrive on the tables, to be put into a cool place, or labelled or ticketed. Recently we have learnt that vouchers for crabs and lobsters and cream cakes are more acceptable than the food itself. Then you can eat them when you want to, or have a luxury cake when you need it.

At 10.30 the children gather in the garden in fancy dress. Sark is good at fancy dress, and it is a popular competition. Elves, fairies, sweeps, wells and Jack, pantomime characters, animals; they all set off along the Avenue to advertise the fair and arrive at the Bel Air in time to welcome one of the star turns of the fair, L'Assemblaie Guernaisiaise – the Guernsey Dancers. These perform traditional dances to an accordion at intervals during the afternoon, but not until they have judged the fancy dress competition.

L'Assemblaie Guernaisiaise demonstrate a traditional dance at the Church Fair.

By 2 pm the stalls are ready and the gates are opened. The stallholders wear the traditional sun-bonnets, aprons and long skirts of a century ago, with shawls if it is not too hot. If it is hot, the sun-bonnets are appreciated. They really do keep you cool, and stallholders need to keep cool! For most of them the afternoon is a blank, they are so busy, but the garden is always crowded and the visitors thoroughly enjoy pitching a real horse shoe, tossing a hay bale or throwing an Elizabethan cannon ball. Strictly speaking, they are Georgian cannon balls, but Elizabethan rolls off the tongue better! There are competitions for children, in which they can win a cuddly toy – puffins in recent years – and many other games requiring a variety of skills. The Traditional Fair is a highlight for people who deliberately time their holidays to coincide with the fair. Even the locals make that Saturday a holiday.

~

Some are lucky enough to have a day off every week. There are no day visitors on a Sunday. On Sunday the only traffic allowed on the road are the tractors doing essential agricultural work, the carrier meeting the one scheduled boat and carriages taking people to church, or to catch the single boat. So carriage drivers have a day off, as do builders, shop keepers and fuel suppliers. Hotels and guest house workers, café and restaurant employees and, of course, farmers and fishermen work as usual.

Local families do make time to take the children down to the sea, however. The Creux Harbour is a favourite spot. There the men (and the boys) will sit for hours on the sea wall, fishing. Before the children could learn to swim in the Petit Champ pool, the harbour was the place for swimming lessons. Jumping off the quay at half-tide, the cliffs echo with the resounding splash as feet hit the waves. On the beach there are picnics waiting for seal-wet little bodies and the harbour café does a roaring trade in ice-cream. On the flat ground between the cliff and the telephone kiosk there are people messing about with boats, tinkering with engines, preparing rowing skiffs.

At intervals local boats come in, perhaps returning fishermen or local charter launches, to tie up and load or unload people, lobsters, wet fish, or just the paraphernalia of a trip in a boat. The Non Pareil and other boats taking tours round the island arrive and depart. Just sitting on the harbour wall and watching the Sunday traffic is a pleasure in itself.

~

The Creux Harbour is usually peaceful and lazy, but the other event that often takes place in August changes all that! On Water Carnival Sunday it is so crowded that the cobbles hardly show between the bodies. The Sark Water Carnival came about because of a crisis in the Professor Saint Medical Fund.

Water Carnival Sunday, and the man-powered flying machines await the start of the revels.

Sark, not being part of the United Kingdom, has no National Health. Medicine and doctor's visits have to be paid for, and so do visits to hospitals. Professor Charles Saint, who lived on Sark, left a large sum of money to set up two funds, a Medical Fund and an

Educational Fund. The Medical Fund was used to subsidise medicines. As drugs became more expensive, so the Fund was less and less able to cope with the demand on it. Then, on an August evening at the pub in 1981, a group of people decided to do something to top up the Professor Saint Medical Fund. They decided to revive the Sark Water Carnival.

There had been a pre-war regatta with swimming races and boat races, and they thought up something along those lines, starting with a parade of decorated boats headed by a Carnival Queen, with the added attraction of a man-powered flying machine to round off the afternoon. Within three weeks they had organised the first of the new series of carnivals, and it is still going!

All the fun of the Water Carnival, reflected in the fast and furious home-made raft race.

The actual date depends on having a suitable tide at a suitable time for the man-powered flying machines to go off the Creux Harbour quay. The very first one was in September, and some have been in July, but the Water Carnival usually takes place in August. The weeks before the actual date are taken up with building things, such as flying machines, structures to fit on boats, bicycles that will cross the harbour, rafts for the raft race, and many other curiosities, all top secret. Visitors are discouraged and people become very taciturn as the date approaches. Building these projects goes on in the evenings and at night; Everyone is at work during the day.

The Water Carnival is a two day event. It begins on a Saturday, when there are plenty of commercial boats running. The first day's frivolities take place on the top of the island, in a field. That day opens with a grand fancy dress procession, open to everyone, visitors and locals alike. They all gather in the Post Office's forecourt and walk along The Avenue to the field in which stalls, games and crazy competitions have been prepared. This began in the field by the Mermaid, but in recent years has moved to the field by the Bel Air at the top of the harbour hill.

Once in the field, the fancy dress is judged, some of the children's costumes making the choice difficult. The losers are cheered by a small prize for taking part! Adult classes vary with the years. In some years there is a large entry, in others much fewer. There are still original ideas turning up, despite the many years of competition.

With the judging over, the rest of the day commences. There is a crèche for children in one corner of the field, to give parents a chance to be daft. Fathers can take part in the Great Egg Throwing Contest. The object of this is to throw, and catch, a raw egg over the greatest possible distance. The record at the time of writing is 202 feet. The egg must, of course, remain in one piece. Many do not.

Mum may indulge in welly-throwing, or both parents may take part in the races. The form of these varies. One year had the competitors running about in jelly-filled flippers. Not easy! There have been dry land skis, overhead water-filled balloons to burst, frames to be climbed, almost every imaginable hazard to be overcome. There are children's races, too, and the ever-present stalls with treasure hunts, wheels of fortune, naming cuddly toys and innumerable opportunities to win teddy bears, dragons or whatever else is fashionable that year. There are food stalls, ice cream stalls, hot dog stands and drinks can be won in many of the games. The last competition is tug-o-war; inter-island, inter-hotel and finally, between gangs of children. It is a good day out, and the ferries returning to Guernsey and the day trips going back to Jersey are full of cheerful, rather noisy passengers who have had a whale of a time.

Meanwhile, back at the field, the stalls, tents, games and everything are struck and moved down to the Creux Harbour to be re-erected, ready for the watery part of the Carnival on Sunday. The harbour has been cleaned and then washed down by the fire brigade, ready for the onslaught. The bunting is in place very quickly and the loudspeakers are connected and ready to go. Tables are put up and everything that can be set up, is.

That evening sees the competition for Miss Sark Water Carnival in the Island Hall. A panel of judges made up of guests from the five hotels makes sure of impartiality, and both local girls, seasonal workers and visitors take part. They parade in dresses, and personality is an important part of their qualifications. The hall is packed for the occasion; there is a band, but very little room to dance! The choice made, Miss Water Carnival is crowned and locals disperse, to finish flying machines, to complete boat decorations or just to sleep after a long, hard day.

Sunday, and people are down at the harbour early to decorate boats, set up stalls and to put out food and drinks. The Creux Harbour is closed for the day to visiting boats, but all the bays and the Maseline Harbour are full of visiting vessels of all shapes and sizes. There are no spare beds at all in Sark on Water Carnival weekend. The transports are allowed to run down the hill that Sunday morning to bring those who cannot walk easily. The events usually begin at about noon, the entry of Miss Water Carnival starting the day. She declares the Carnival open and the procession of decorated boats sweeps into the picturesque harbour.

Some people elect to watch the fun from the restaurant set up on the pier-head across the harbour mouth. Champagne and lobster after a lift across in a bo'sun's chair! Sometimes the gourmets finish with a plunge into the sea at the end.

The scene is always enchanting, with the towering cliffs making a backdrop to excited crowds surrounding a translucent green sea. The boats, with flowers, scenes from the past – from fairytales, from pop songs, from natural history or legend – circle the harbour as the judges get to work. It makes a good opening. Sometimes the decorated boats interact with the crowds. The Viking boat repeated its rape and pillage raid at home, with equal success. A mini Sark Trader hurled its cargo to people on the quay. Whatever the result, everyone enjoys the contest!

After the decorated boats, anything can happen. There are swimming races, races to see how many people will fit into a yak and cross the harbour, a cross-harbour bicycle race, a water-tourney, with mops instead of lances, there are battles on the greasy pole, home-made raft races and costumed aqua-leaping. Once we had synchronised swimming, and the team managed it very well. The events are not always the same, but they are always lively, and the highlight of the day is the man-powered flying machine competition.

No one has really succeeded in flying, although some of the hang glider designs came dangerously near a successful flight. The work put into the machines is considerable, and replicas are very carefully researched. There have been a variety of 'planes, a flying bedstead, a crane (just guess which year that was) a flying nurse, a dinosaur, a toad, a flying elephant, a Spaceship Enterprise and innumerable rockets. There have been whirling propellers, spitting exhaust rockets, tickets sold by Miss Piggy, a fleet of Red Arrows. There has been no end to the ingenuity and effort put in by would-be flyers to finish the Carnival afternoon in style – even with a bang in some cases.

The last event finished, the cups and prizes presented by Miss Water Carnival and the work starts again. Down come the loudspeakers and the bunting, the tables are stacked on to trailers, the rubbish is cleared up and by Monday morning the Creux Harbour sinks back into its sleepy summer image. The Carnival is over for another year.

The Carnival may be over, but there is no peace – presumably we're wicked – because the next event is upon us. It's time to get the ex-hibits ready for the Grand Autumn Show.

~

The Autumn Show is the agricultural one, when the farmers and cooks get a chance to join the gardeners in displaying their skills. There are classes for agricultural roots, cereals, kale and collections of seeds as well as dairy produce. There are also classes for garden vegetables, autumn flowers and a variety of breads, cakes and preserves. The tables are covered by gleaming white cloths, and the exhibits spread out over three rooms in the Island Hall. There are flower arrangements, miniature gardens (from adults in this show), displays from nature and dried flowers to provide decoration alongside the incredible variety of dahlias.

The kitchens of the island have been worked overtime to supply the victoria sponges (there are men's and children's classes for them as well) fruit cakes, plain sweet cakes, meringues, the local specialities like gâche and apple cake and that catch-all of gastronomic delights, the any extras class. The decorative icing has an enthusiastic entry from the children and more painstaking ones from the adults. There is a chance for everyone to have a go. The scent of fresh baking ensures that the Hall does a roaring trade in snacks!

The Autumn Show is at the end of August, and it means that the end of the season is in sight. By this time of year, the Sark residents are getting a bit worn, particularly if the summer has been hot. 1976 was a killer season, what with worrying about the animals in fields that looked like doormats and soaking carriage wheels overnight in turn to make sure that the spokes didn't shrink too much in the heat and pop out of the wheel. That year our noses never stopped peeling, our eyes were sore from the dust and we couldn't even soak in a bath at the end of the day to get rid of the tension. The end of August was a landmark; we could survive until the gales!

~

CREUX HARBOUR

SEPTEMBER

SEPTEMBER BEGINS WITH THE HARVEST Festival in St Peter's Church where the light standards are sheathed in corn and the front of the pulpit disappears behind wheat, barley and oats. There are plenty of root vegetables, tomatoes and other vegetables from the show to cover the window sills, pile up round the font and lodge in any available space. There is a loaf in the shape of a sheaf and a plate of grapes on the altar and freshly cooked crabs and lobsters next to local cream, butter and eggs on the table in front of the pews. Nothing is forgotten, there is a bundle of gorse sticks and a bag of coal in the church porch.

The harvest is very obvious on Sark and we really can give thanks for our crops, our produce and our very beautiful surroundings. Even the hedgerows give us plentiful blackberries to make into pies, crumbles, jams, jellies and vinegars. Who can help being thankful for the fresh food, the comfort of being part of a community and, to crown it all, magnificent sunrises and sunsets, long sweeps of cliffs with waves like lace trimming along their bases, wind-bent trees and salt-scented air. The Harvest Festival is a popular service; people take the opportunity to voice appreciation of a very good life.

St. Peter's Church decorated for the Harvest Festival, with corn and maize round the lamp standards and in the windows.

Visitors are still on Sark at the beginning of September, although with the end of the school holidays approaching the really crowded days have passed. Many come to the Harvest Festival to remind themselves of the services of the past, when British harvests, even in towns, had more fresh produce from allotments and gardens. They enjoy the close contact with farming and fishing, but they also enjoy visiting a church that looks and feels as if it is used and looked after. We are used to popping in and out of the building for a variety of reasons, but many visitors still regard churches as dim, dusty buildings for funerals and weddings. The cheerful, comfortable atmosphere is noticed by the many day visitors who go in because that is what you do when you are on a holiday trip and come out saying, 'What a lovely little Church!'

The outside is rather stark, a late Georgian oblong with a chancel added by W T Collings in 1900 and a tower built by the island. That means that the Anglican Church owns the body of the church, the Seigneur owns the chancel and the island is responsible for the tower, the housing of the bell and the bell itself. It makes repair bills very complicated! The inside has the boxed pews which are rented by tenants and certain families, within cream-washed, two-foot-thick walls and, recessed into the walls, some very attractive stained glass windows. Until 1979 the wooden seats were mostly bare and the kneelers shabby. Then a new priest was appointed who regenerated the community's care for the parish church.

The inside was made more attractive – and more comfortable – with hand-embroidered cushions and kneelers. That really was an island effort. 109 people helped, from the schoolchildren to the older residents. At first the patterns were bought and worked, but as confidence grew we designed our own. The Ladies Guild organised the work, and still meets on Tuesdays throughout the winter to make things for their stall at the Traditional Fair.

Earlier they also made the panels at the back of the church that illustrate the island's history, recording the early monastery that was sited at the present Seigneurie until the Black Death killed most of the population. It records the granting of the charter to Helier de Carteret in 1565, the sale to the Le Pelleys, the disastrous venture into silver mining by the Le Pelleys, the eventual passing of the island into the hands of the Collings family (Collings was the Dame's maiden name) right up to the Royal visit of 1957, when La Dame created a precedent, the first Dame to kneel and swear loyalty to a Queen. There was no record at all of a woman swearing loyalty to a woman; the ceremony was adapted from the seigneur's swearing to be the liege man of the monarch.

All this combines to make the church a pleasant surprise to day visitors and the place to be on a Sunday morning for resident visitors. Those who are on Sark for the great festivals enjoy taking part in services which are still closely allied to the old Book of Common Prayer. Residents and visitors alike sit among the apples, tomatoes and corn and sing the traditional hymns with gusto.

After the Harvest Festival the perishable gifts are auctioned off for Church funds. The crabs, lobsters, butter, cream and home-made harvest cakes are much sought after and there is a lively half hour on the small forecourt as bids echo round the circle of people. The balance of the gifts are parcelled up into boxes and given to the sick and the older residents.

~

The annual Horse Show is the last major event in the Sark season; that is held on the first Monday in the month. The show was begun in the 1930s by the Dame and the first one was organised by her daughter Douce. It was held at the beginning of the season then, to make sure that the carriages were all fit for the road. The need to check on carriages went when the licensing system was introduced. They could not go on the road unless they were sound! The Horse Show moved to the end of the season.

The weekend before the show is busy with youngsters grooming horses and drivers crawling under and round their carriages to remove the dirt of the season. The judges inspect everything, including the turntable under the driver's seat where the horse-hair and dust cling to the grease – the whole lot has to be cleaned off and regreased. The harness has to be dismantled, the leather oiled and polished and the brass or chrome cleaned. From under the residue of a season's work the animals and vehicles emerge resplendent on Monday morning, ready to compete with their companions of the road.

The Clos de Milieu, better known as the Horse Show field, is picturesque, fringed with trees and brambles carrying a rich crop of ripe blackberries. The tent and the roped enclosures are usually taken to the field on Saturday and put up on Sunday. The Horse Show has been blessed with good weather for years. The sun is low, its rays edging the leaves and the grass with gold and shining on the gleaming carriages and glossy horses waiting in the shade at the west end of the field. The slanting light catches the insects, gold motes dancing above the grass as the horses' hooves disturb them. The swallows are still with us and they swoop low across the grass between the horses and humans, catching the insects, building up reserves to last them on their long southward flight.

Spectators arrive to seat themselves on chairs, hay bales, shooting sticks or rugs and refresh themselves from the abundant supply of home-made quiches, sandwiches, cakes and tea or coffee in the tent. The stop-me-and-buy-one tricycle has icecream to help people to keep cool, or they may buy Sark's home-made ice cream, made from the dark yellow local cream.

On the field the show begins with the horses on bridle. Some of the horses sense the occasion, and arch their necks, stepping out to impress the judges, who come from Jersey and Guernsey.

Horses on bridle are followed by the vehicle classes, two-wheelers, victorias, vans, wagonettes and box carts, in pristine condition, driven by bowler-hatted drivers with lap rugs and whips held at 45°, unrecognisable as the vehicles that wait at the top of the harbour hill.

Not all the vehicles are out every day, some are kept for special occasions. Johnny de Carteret's beautiful victoria is kept for weddings, Royal visits and similar celebrations. It has won the Silver Cup for the best turnout many times, but not every time. Karen Godwin's smart van has taken the prize on other occasions.

The afternoon ends with the races, when the patient carriage horses get a chance to gallop while their riders, bareback, put hats on hardy human posts standing immobile as the horses gallop round them. The riders bob for apples, dress up, race and generally enjoy themselves. So do the horses! Dressage rider Carl Hester rode in his first show on Sark long before he left in 1985 to begin his training with Jenny Lorriston-Clark. He lived here, went to school here and began his now distinguished career with the wild rides that finish the Horse Show.

Johnny de Carteret driving his victoria at the Sark Horse Show, where he won the cup for the Best Turnout.

By the time the sun sinks below the trees, the judging is over, the cups and prizes are presented and the visitors have left to have a drink before they catch the last ferry back to Guernsey. On the field the ropes and posts vanish, the tent is struck and packed up while it is still dry and the horses and carriages head for the farms and stables carry-ing tired but happy passengers. The last Sark event of the season is over.

~

Now the children go back to school, to start another year's work. In the Infants, new pupils settle in, having spent a few afternoons there in the previous term to take away the strangeness. The most painful partings are for those families with children going to school off the island, so that they can take qualifying exams. Elizabeth College, the public school in Guernsey, is obliged by its charter from Queen Elizabeth I to provide places for Sark boys, and some go there. They are the lucky ones.

For children brought up in a community in which they know everyone and everyone knows them, it is a shock to leave home and go to a town full of strangers. It takes them some time to adjust, and a few don't. They come home, unable to work through their desperate homesickness. At Elizabeth College, there are older Sark boys to comfort the new ones, and the break is not quite so hard. Also, being in Guernsey, the teachers understand the boys' background and can help them. New interests, new friends and a busy timetable helps to keep the initial misery at bay. It is the parents who suffer, worrying about the children's welfare and anxiously waiting for half term, when they can come home again.

~

The annual visit of the Sir William Arnold, the Guernsey lifeboat, takes place in late August or September. The lifeboat is an important part of the island's life, taking patients to hospital in Guernsey if the weather is too wild for the St John's ambulance launch, the *Flying Christine II*, to make the crossing. It spends the day in the Creux Harbour, taking people for rides along the east coast of Sark. The throb of the powerful engines make the deck shake underfoot and the coast hurtles past at an incredible rate, the wake creaming the aquamarine sea behind the boat. The RLNI is another cause to which Sark makes generous donations. You never know when it will be you on board, as a shipwrecked mariner or as a patient!

~

Battle of Britain means a lot on an island that was occupied, and Sark supports the RAF Benevolent Fund generously. The annual Battle of Britain Show, in September, has a fly-past by the Memorial Flight, a procession of 'planes, old and new, and a display by the Red Arrows. They perform above St Peter Port harbour, surely one of the most beautiful of all their sites.

The 'planes are not allowed to fly over Sark, but they spend the night in Jersey and fly up to Guernsey to give a morning display, and every 'plane circles Sark at least once, acknowledging the fund-raising done on Sark for them. On a clear day there is a spectacular view of the display over St Peter Port from the Eperquerie or, if you are lucky, from the Seigneurie tower. Clear days are few and far between, however, and in many years Sark has to be content with a flash of red, white and blue smoke from the Red Arrows as they hurtle overhead from Alderney, headed for Jersey, refuelling and an afternoon display.

In November 1942 a Lancaster crash-landed in Sark and fifty years later, on Battle of Britain day, CTV, the local television station, brought the pilot back to see where his unlucky journey had ended. Flight Sergeant Eric Singleton had been flying back from a raid on Stuttgart in a damaged 'plane, his crew instructed to bail out while he fought with faulty controls. The rear gunner was still in his blister and there was another crew member in the body of the 'plane, which was damaged by a flare. Flt Sgt Singleton, off course with instruments not working properly, survived the flak from Jersey, and saw below him a small island. He thought it was the Scillies. The rear gunner, who returned to Sark in 1979, thought it was the Isle of Wight.

Flt Sgt Singleton saw what looked like a landing strip, and brought down the disabled 'plane, to find that what resembled a hedge was in fact a solid earthen bank. The 'plane goudged out the top of the bank – the holes are still there to prove it – and crashed into the smaller field beyond. The three men climbed out of the 'plane, heard what they thought was the Home Guard crashing about in the dark, then found, to their horror, that they had landed on occupied Sark. They were marched to the German headquarters in the Manoir in the dark and shipped off to Guernsey. They finished the war in a prison camp in Germany.

Eric Singleton was amazed to find that there were a few mangled bits of his Lancaster still in the field – called the aeroplane field because a small light aircraft landed there in the carefree prewar days! – and he was able to take a souvenir away with him. There wasn't much left. Metal and bolts were in very short supply on occupied Sark and, however hard the Germans tried, the 'plane slowly vanished to leave a few twisted bars under a tangle of brambles.

In September 1992, on Battle of Britain Day, Flt Sgt Singleton was standing in the aeroplane field when the Lancaster and Hurricane of the Memorial Flight flew over Sark, with Chief Pleas' permission, and saluted the pilot who crash-landed a Lancaster there fifty years before. Eric Singleton said nothing so wonderful had ever happened to him before.

~

If the equinoctial gales stay away, there are still visitors on the island, but the boat schedules change in September to three return trips a week, from six return trips a day! In 1981 Max Bygraves actually came to Sark, to the delight of Mrs Retta Roberts, one of his most ardent fans. He had his photo taken with her and it is now a prized possesion! Home Secretaries usually visit Sark during their term of Office, and they often come in September. Leon Brittan and Douglas Hurd have both inspected the minuscule prison with its spartan cells. Prisoners can only be kept in the iron-barred stone cells for two days; longer sentences are served in Guernsey.

With less horse traffic on the roads, jobs that obstruct them can be done before the weather gets too bad. One very important task in recent years was the replacement of the housing of the school bell. The wood of the small bell tower was found to be dangerously rotten when a roof repair was carried out. So up came the crane from the harbour and the bell and tower were carefully removed. The bell proved to be a revelation. It has a inscription on it, which reads:

DE PAR MONsr DE St OUIAN 1580

The bell was given to Sark by the Seigneur of St Ouen in Jersey in 1580. At that time the Seigneur of St Ouen was also the Seigneur of Sark, the first one, Helier de Carteret. This bell had been hung in a field behind the present church of St Peter's. The field's name is still

Clos de la Tour de la Cloche, or the Bell Tower field. It was rung to warn people of attack or in any emergency. It became the school bell in 1820.

A bell expert visited the island while it was still on the ground, and told us that it was probably cast in Normandy. There are leaf decorations round the top of the bell; the expert said that he had never seen anything like them before. The crane reappeared to put the new bell tower and its historic bell back on top of the school building.

~

The useful crane was used for a very unusual job a couple of Septembers later. A Sark resident bought a swimming pool, ready made, 15 feet wide. It was delivered by cargo boat and sat on the Maseline Harbour quay. First problem. It was too wide to go through the Maseline tunnel. However, it was a swimming pool, and so it was water- tight. It was put back into the sea and sailed round to the bottom of the harbour hill, between the two harbours, and the crane lifted out of the water on to a trailer. It was through the tunnel! It was towed up the harbour hill to the top. Second problem. It was too wide to get round the tight bend by the power station. The crane duly lifted it over the sharp corner and it spent the night in the lay-by at the top of the hill.

Very early the next morning, before it was light, the journey continued, so that the road would be clear when the horses came out. The swimming pool moved north along the Rue Lucas. Problem three. The stone gatepost at Le Carrefour which projects into the road from the old cottage. The width of the road at that point is less than 15 feet. The crane could be used once again to lift the pool over the gatepost and round the tight corner, except for problem four. There were telephone wires all over the corner, the crane couldn't lift the pool high enough. Pause while Sark's telephone engineer was summoned from his bed to take down the wires. The journey

Opposite: The new belfry, containing its very old bell, is lowered into position above the Senior School, seat of Chief Pleas, Sark's parliament.

was then able to start again.

By this time it was light and the carriage drivers were going to fetch their horses. Luckily there were no more hitches in the road, the pool progressed slowly but surely up La Rue du Sermon, round the Clos à Jaon corner and into the Seigneurie road. It reached its destination at the north of the island. Fifth problem. The gate was too narrow to allow the pool through to the building site. The crane was called into use again, this time to lift it over first one hedge, then a second and finally to lower it into the hole in the ground. Sark had one more swimming pool. The crane had proved its worth yet again and the horses met no problems on their island tour.

~

Towards the end of the month, hotels have last night dinners to give locals a chance of a final dinner out, then they start to close in succession, except for Dixcart, which has stayed open in recent years. Carriage drivers leave to return to college or to take up winter jobs. The Avenue is suddenly negotiable again. Most of the faces are familiar, and we have time to stop and chat, to find out what has happened during the summer, and to think about the winter season, now within planning distance. People heave a sigh and relax a bit!

~

THE MONK'S WELL
IN THE SEIGNEURIE GROUNDS

OCTOBER

THE SEASON IS DEFINITELY ON its last legs in October, even if the gales don't disrupt the boats. The evenings are pulling in, all the migrant birds are gone or getting ready to go, the hotels are closed, the staff have left and Sark turns to its winter pursuits. The societies reawaken with AGMs and election of officers, the Theatre Group decides on its annual production, and the Michaelmas Chief Pleas sits. In Medieval England, Michaelmas was the time for financial settlements; rent day, the day when tithes were collected. Sark continued to work to its medieval financial year until 1982, and *tenants* still pay the Seigneur their *rentes* at the Michaelmas Chief Pleas. They also pay their pew rents.

Sark must be the last place in the British Isles to have rented pews in the parish church. Traditionally, some of the *tenements* have pews attached to them, while others belong to families who were once *tenants* but have sold their *tenements* while keeping their pews. Not all the pews are rented. There are public pews at the back of the church, which are open. The rented pews are boxed, near the front.

In practice no one minds where people sit in church, but on formal occasions, such as the installation of the incumbent or a Royal visit, people sit in their own pews and the churchwardens will ask the owners permission to seat other people in their pews.

Rentes are settled before the Chief Pleas meeting, the tenants taking them up to the Seigneur as he sits on the dais at the end of the schoolroom. At the Michaelmas Chief Pleas the new Constable and Vingtenier are elected. Sark does not have paid policemen. Each able bodied man will serve first as Vingtenier for a year, then as Constable for one year. The job is not simply that of a policeman. The Constable plays an important part in the administration of the island, collecting taxes, supervising road repairs and generally working with the Douzaine. He also has the unenviable task of organising the Sark side of any Royal visit, liaising with the Guernsey police and the Royal security men.

~

Sark very rarely has any crime. In such a close community it is difficult to get away with much! There was one colourful character who stole something at the end of every year, leaving the evidence where it could not be missed, so that he could spend most of the winter in gaol. Prison in Guernsey was warm and well fed! He stopped doing it when he was told that the next offence would send him to an English prison.

Otherwise there are drunken arguments to disturb the winter peace, but very little else. Summer is a bit more hectic these days. Summer workers sometimes bring drugs into the island, and they are always amazed at the speed with which they are discovered.

One young tearaway took a job as a kitchen porter, arrived on a Friday, went to the Mermaid on Friday night and got rather drunk, then broke into a shop to steal cash and clothes. The theft was reported early on Saturday morning and by lunchtime the thief was in the hands of the Constable and the stolen goods recovered. Coming from an anonymous town, the youth didn't realise that, as a stranger, people noticed what he was doing, where and when he went home, which route he took. When the theft was reported, the Constable had no problem in discovering his name and found the stolen goods under his bed. He was the only stranger to walk that way that evening, and no local would have stolen clothes that could instantly be recognised if they wore them.

Seigneur Mr Michael Beaumont points out an interesting feature of the old Arsenal, while standing in front of Sark's tiny prison. Jersey's Lieutenant-Governor Sir Peter Whiteley, is asking the question, while Guernsey's Lieutenant-Governor, Sir Peter Le Cheminant, looks on.

He was brought before the Seneschal's court, which at that time sat in the Senior School during the children's lunch hour. He kept asking when he was going to a proper court, obviously bewildered by the speed and lack of uniforms, and certainly not grasping the fact that Sark is not part of the English legal system. He did know what a 'proper court' should be like. When the Constable contacted his home town in the Midlands, it turned out that he had dozens of convictions for petty theft and drugs, and that he rarely bothered to work. He was kept in the Sark prison that night and deported as soon as possible after that, forbidden to return to Sark for three years. He never did understand how such an apparently sleepy little island dealt with him so quickly.

The retiring Constable heaves a sigh of relief at the Michaelmas Chief Pleas, knowing that his two years are over. He will not be expected to serve again.

~

The Michaelmas Chief Pleas decides on the rate of taxation for the following year, decides on the amount of money to be spent on road repairs through the winter and committees are brought up to strength. The house discusses the schedule, fares and freight rates of the Isle of Sark Shipping Company vessels and decides on any changes in time for the printed timetables to be ready for the winter enquiries.

The *Procureur des Pauvres*, who looks after those islanders who are in need of help, is elected to serve a two-year term, as is the Deputy Procureur. The Deputy Procureur is usually elected Procureur and a retiring Constable is often elected Deputy. All these posts are honorary. Sark works on co-operation rather than bureaucracy.

The new Constable and Vingtenier join the Douzaine for their next job, which is to visit all the harbours and walk all the roads to decide on winter repairs. It's called the funeral march, and it takes place on a Saturday after Chief Pleas. The fourteen men split up into smaller groups, each taking a part of the island. They check that people are keeping their banks tidy and weed-free and their trees cut back from the road at the same time. The *branchage* that is called, and there is a notice posted in the island boxes warning people of when it will take place.

The boat schedules change again, with only one early boat a week, and again at the end of the month to the winter service, with in and out boats bringing post for four days and shopping trips on

Wednesdays and Saturdays, and we have to learn when the post closes all over again. Post is linked to boats, so if you can remember which day it is and what the sailing pattern for that day is, you know that the post closes an hour before the last boat leaves. Complicated? Well, you do get used to it after a week or so!

~

October is a popular month for local weddings, with the season finished but with boats every day to allow guests to get to Sark easily. An island wedding touches almost every one in the community. Those who are not guests will certainly either come to church or stand outside. The carriage owners each give a carriage for the wedding party, with rosettes of ribbon, matching the bridesmaids' dresses, bows and flowers decorating the victorias and other carriages. Owners work hard to make their carriage look lovely for the big day. The church flower ladies transform the inside of the church into a flower garden and the cake is usually made and decorated on Sark.

Inside the church, the choir launder their surplices and sing with a will. After the marriage service the bride and groom may leave the church under an appropriate arch; a recent wedding had an arch of decorated driving whips. The carriages drive along The Avenue to give everyone a chance to see the bride, and the reception may be at home, in the Island Hall or at a hotel. Truly Sark weddings use the Island Hall; nowhere else is big enough for the family!

After the reception, the bride and groom, with bridesmaids, best man, ushers and a number of guests, take wedding cake and wine, pile into the carriages and drive round the island taking cake and wine to those who could not get to the wedding. Then, in the evening, there is usually a party or a dance to round off the day. The bride and groom leave the island for their honeymoon the following day.

That is always supposing that the boats are not disrupted by wind. For those going away, the most difficult part of the journey is the beginning. Weather forecasts are watched carefully, and the journey started a day early if there are crucial flight connections to be made. There are two hazards: wind, which will upset the boat

schedules, and fog, which holds up the 'planes. In October, if one doesn't stop you, the other will!

For those not planning to fly anywhere, fog is not a problem. The boats are equipped with excellent radar and fog, however thick, does not stop them. Wind is a nuisance to everyone. Toiling along on a bike against a permanent head wind is very tiring. It's remarkable that whichever way you cycle, the wind is against you. It eddies and swirls about, a malignant force determined to slow you down. October is usually quite windy, and it was in October that the great hurricane hit us in 1987.

~

The hurricane arrived overnight on Friday 16th October. The weather was strange on Thursday evening. Thursday is the church choir practice night, and the choir went into church at 7 o'clock on a fairly normal, damp autumn evening. When they came out just after 8 o'clock, they discovered something very strange. The outside of the glass on the church doors was running with moisture, just as the inside of windows stream on a very cold day. Stepping from the church into the open air was like walking into a tropical greenhouse. The air was warm and wet, and very still. It felt ominous. It was.

During the night, the wind rose rapidly until it was screaming through the trees and the chimneys. There was the sound of crashing as trees, still covered with leaves, were torn out of earth softened beforehand by rain, their roots not able to stand the force of the wind on the foliage. Roofs were lifted, doors blew open and off, windows were blown in; all this on an island designed for high winds. Sark houses are tucked into valleys or reinforced against winter storms. Being virtually a rock sticking up from the sea, we expect to be wind-blown.

Waking up at about 3 o'clock in the morning, the sound was just like that of a wartime bombing raid – and provoked a long-forgotten reaction, 'Well, I can't stop it, I'll go back to sleep'.

Opposite: A Sark wedding, the victoria decorated with flowers, rosettes and ribbons for the occasion.

Early on the following morning the chaos was revealed. The sun came up at about 7 o'clock on a world transformed in just 12 hours. There were trees completely surrounding La Seigneurie. Every path was blocked and it was necessary to climb out. There were ten trees across the road in the hundred or so yards between the big main gate and the southerly farm gate. The rest of the island was the same. Every man turned out to help make the roads passable. The crane came up from the harbour to lift heavy trunks from across the lanes. The air smelt of leaf sap from the mangled leaves, of green blood from all the damaged trees. What was so heart-breaking was that it was the healthy, leafy trees that had gone. The stark wooden skeletons

The cleaning-up after the hurricane is still going on. Here the great oak in the Seigneurie grounds is reduced to planks.

left by Dutch Elm disease were still standing, most of them, the wind not exerting enough force on their leafless branches to push them over.

Amazingly, in all this plant destruction, the only animal killed was an old Muscovy duck. A tree fell on him by the Seigneurie pond. No humans were hurt, and when stock was taken, the damage to buildings was not too bad. It was not the same story at sea level. There must have been an aerial maelstrom in the Creux Harbour. The dinghies were smashed, a side of one of them coming to rest halfway up the 200 foot cliffs. Two beautiful fishing boats were lost, virtually without trace. The engine of one was found, well away from its moorings, and a stem post of the other. Unfairly, it was the firm moorings that destroyed the boats. Boats with moorings that had dragged were waterlogged, but could just about be salvaged.

The scars of that savage storm were with us for some time. Standing on the Hog's Back and looking up Dixcart valley, the course of the wind was obvious. There was a path of fallen trees, looking for all the world like spilled matches, the direction of their falling marking the eddies of the storm path. After a day the plants on the cliffs and côtils turned black, seared by the salt spray whipped up from the sea. Lovely, green Sark looked as though it had gone into mourning for the death of so many trees.

The trees were not wasted. A planking machine was brought over to the island and what wood could be saved, was saved. The massive old oak that had grown in front of La Seigneurie became cannon mounts for the cannon round the island, became a castle for children to climb into in the middle of a maze in the Seigneurie gardens, other oaks became the ribs of boats built on the island, one to replace one of the lost fishing boats. Several things were made that would not have been if expensive wood had had to be imported from the mainland.

The island views certainly changed. Suddenly the sea appeared across banks and hedges, turns in paths gave sweeping vistas down valleys and houses appeared on horizons which had been tree-covered. People began replanting immediately, and in time Sark will regain the protection of sheltering trees. In the interim, cycling is much harder work!

If the storm had hit just a fortnight later, the story in the harbour might have been different. By then many of the boats would have been out of the water. After the end of October, it is illegal to take shellfish from Sark waters. The quays fill up with strings of lobster pots as the fishermen bring them in and put them ashore. The long lines slowly disappear as they go into a store or up the hill to be repaired. The crane lifts steadily until even the hardiest fisherman has his boat on the quay or in a field. Some have smaller boats that they can drop into the water on a quiet day for some wet fishing, but most fishermen have winter jobs to go to; they become builders, road menders or odd job men until the end of March, when the potting season opens again.

Those who stay on Sark begin the winter work. There is time to have dinner parties at home again, the Ladies Guild return to their embroidery, the tap dance, aerobics, badminton, music society, chess club, and all the other winter pastimes begin. The pubs have meat draws on a Friday night. The community settles down to enjoy the quiet months.

~

ST. PETER'S CHURCH

NOVEMBER

NOT A SEASON OF MISTS and mellow fruitfulness, but a season of fogs and speedy windiness. Autumn glory is rare on an island as windy as this. The leaves do not get a chance to change colour and provide red, brown and yellow arches over the lanes. As soon as they go brown they are whirled away from the twigs. We do get drifts of dry leaves along the banks if it doesn't rain too much, but no one would come to Sark to admire the autumn show.

November is holiday time for Sark people, a good month to be elsewhere, away from mud, dripping branches and post interrupted either because the fog keeps the 'planes away from Guernsey or because the winds keep the boats away from Sark.

~

It begins with bonfire night, however. That's called Budlo Night on Sark. Same pattern as England, different name. After all, Guy Fawkes was nothing to do with the Channel Islands! Not the same parliament! Same king, but he escaped harm. Whatever it's called, Sark has a bonfire night and burns an effigy – well, several effigies actually, as there is usually a Guy Fawkes competition among the schoolchildren. There is no 'penny for the guy' tradition here, however. The guys are usually well made, or they don't stand a chance of a prize; they do burn well!

Bonfire night is very weather-dependent. It has taken place on clear, still evenings when the fireworks soar up over the sea from the biggest party at the north of the island, bursting against a scatter of autumn stars. On nights like that, the Guernsey fireworks are clearly seen in Sark, giant dandelions of light hanging over the black silhouette across a glimmering sea. Quite beautiful. There are other nights when the wind takes the rockets away at high speed and the bonfire sparks speed across the sky like mini-meteors. The local firemen are always in attendance, keeping an eye on errant ash, just in case!

There are also nights when the fireworks shoot up above the clouds, the bursts softened and dimmed by enshrouding mist. Out-of-time boat flares cast a red glow over the cloudy canopy, giving a weird, witchy quality to the scene. If the mists are lower, the flickering fire makes the shadows of the trees dance black in an orange-coloured haze, or the trees form a lacework of black branches about a glow in a hollow, the children black silhouettes crossing the flames and the fireworks like a sparkle of froth over the bowl of firelight.

Food plays an important part in the evening; home-made soup, sausage rolls, quiche, apple strudel and hot chocolate to warm chilly fingers. Needless to say, there is a charity somewhere on the scene. These vary. They may be national, the RNLI or the Red Cross, or local, for the St John Ambulance launch, the *Flying Christine II*, the School Fund or for the Sark Playgroup.

~

The next event is Remembrance Sunday. That has a great significance on an island that was occupied in World War II and lost fifteen men in the First World War. That may not seem many, but it was almost all the young men in the community. Most of them were serving with the Guernsey Royal Light Infantry, which was virtually wiped out. The War Memorial in front of St Peter's Church bears silent testi-mony, so many of the surnames the same.

If the weather is good, the Remembrance Day service begins outside St Peter's Church, with the choir lined up beside the memorial and the British Legion and the Royal Antediluvian Order of Buffaloes marching up the road from the Island Hall. The wreaths are laid, one by the Seigneur on behalf of the island, one from the British Legion, one from the British Red Cross and one from the RAOB. The names are read out and the silence observed. St Peter's church clock is a little eccentric in its striking, so the two minutes silence is usually timed from a watch.

Remembrance Day and the British Red Cross wreath is laid on the War Memorial outside St. Peter's Church.

The silence on Sark is profound. It is only interrupted by birdsong; the chatter of an alarmed blackbird, the cry of seagulls wheeling overhead, or the distant lowing of a cow. The wind ruffles the hair of the waiting congregation, the surplices of the choir and the British Legion Banner. That went to the Albert Hall in 1985, to be paraded before the Queen in the hands of standard bearer Pat Taylor. We were all very proud of the honour.

If the weather is too windy or wet, the service begins inside the church, grouped round the Memorial window. The address may be from one of the lay readers who were on Sark during the Occupation. The lay readers kept the Sark church going then. There was no priest on the island, one came across from Guernsey for christenings, marriages and funerals, and consecrated wafers and wine so that the lay readers could hold a communion service. These staunch souls get fewer and fewer as the years go by.

After the service the wreaths are weighted down at the base of the War Memorial with a couple of big boulders and some string. Otherwise they fly off along the road in the ever-present wind!

~

November is the start of maintenance of island roads and properties. It's the month for the employment of the road men. One of Sark's winter problems is work. There is no shortage in the summer, but by November the fishermen's boats are out of the water, the day visitors are few and far between, so no extra drivers are needed, in fact, many of the horses have their shoes removed and go out to grass for four months. So the island employs a number of people to repair the roads. Not always men, either. Women have turned their hands to rock breaking at various times. 1987 was the last time a woman worked on the roads.

This form of road repair is fairly recent. Before 1957 the roads were repaired by *La Corvée*. Everyone was expected to give a number of days a year to road repair. Those who could afford it paid someone else to do their road repair service for them. Then the island took over the work and instituted the present system.

The rock for the roads comes from various quarries. One source is the rock alongside the road to the Maseline harbour. This has been blasted back slowly to make room for a trailer park below the island's rubbish collection site. One Tuesday in November 1982 was set aside for a blasting at this rock face. A specialist from Guernsey came over to set the charges. That was why it was on a Tuesday; it was the shopping trip day in 1982 and he came in on the morning boat.

The charge was set, the plunger went down and bang – the charge was alongside a fault line and a great cloud of boulders shot out of the cliff, exploded across the road and swept the sea wall with it into the sea. The road to the harbour was blocked, and it was only with the help of the single JCB on the island that a path was made through the rubble to let the shoppers returning from Guernsey on the afternoon boat through from the Maseline quay. The rock was eventually broken into smaller pieces and put into the crusher for use on the roads. The sea wall had to be rebuilt!

Some of the men who are not employed by the island go to Britain to work on the Christmas trees. A company which sends Christmas trees all over the world is managed by people living on Sark, and for a few weeks before Christmas men are employed to cut and process the trees. The piece work rates are good money for Sark men, who do not have to pay income tax, and at the end of November the younger men set off for some hard living and hard work in the conifer plantations.

The winter's work is not confined to the roads and trees. In November 1987 strange cylindrical shapes arrived and sat at the top of the harbour hill. Chief Pleas had decided that the old methods of sewage disposal were not acceptable with increasing tourist arrivals, and that the island should have a sewage plant. The journey of the large tanks through the narrow twisting lane to the site near Les Lâches was interesting – but it all got there!

Today Sark is the only state to process all its sewage before the clean effluent runs down into the sea and a dry fertilizer can be used for the land. It did not happen straight away. There was a long period with teething troubles, and there is still a hiccough or two today, but the principle has been accepted, and the water sources are noticably cleaner!

November was very busy in 1987; the weather was calm enough for the regilding of the four faces of the church clock and of the weathercock on the top of the tower. A specialist came to the island to do the job, and brought down the cock to reveal a very attractive bird. Up at the top of the tower the details are impossible to see, but propped up by the church door both his size and arrogant head and tail were impressive. Shining with gold leaf, he went back up to the top of the tower, where he looks particularly spectacular in the late afternoon and a south-westerly wind. The flash as he swings with the gusts looks like a lighthouse!

November was the month in which we were able to say farewell to the inside of our lighthouse, Point Robert. Built in 1912, it was classed as a rock-light. It was the only rock light from which the Trinity House crew could pop out to the pub when they were off-duty. The fittings inside were beautiful, all Edwardian wood, brass and glass. The lighthouse was open to visitors in the summer; they enjoyed seeing the highly polished wood and brass, the quaint compass above the rotating lenses and the rainbow light through the curved, bevelled glass, the black-painted iron-work and the gleaming mechanisms for turning the light.

Locals did climb down the long flight of steps to keep in touch and to enjoy the view over the Maseline Harbour and the Burons, but not that often. When automation crept up in 1993, however, and the Head Keeper invited islanders to see the changes in the equipment, the lighthouse men had a busy afternoon. As luck would have it, Sark's learned Society, La Société Serquiaise, had visited Point Robert in February before automation began, and so were able to see the difference. Most of the old equipment was still in place, because it was too difficult and expensive to move it out, but nasty grey boxes full of electronic devices were in place, waiting to take over from the men.

There was a touch of history among the visitors. When the lighthouse was opened in 1912, Miss Retta Perrée, a babe in arms, was taken to it by her mother. Her grand-daughter, eight-year-old Miss Retta Plummer, was among the last visitors in November 1993, and went home to tell her grandmother all about it.

The Trinity House men were very much part of the community. Some of them met and married Sark girls and settled down on the island. They presented a Trinity House flag to hang in St Peter's Church alongside the White Ensign from Sark's adopted boat, the non-ferrous minesweeper *HMS Walkerton*, now mothballed. They entered local shows and took part in carnivals in their spare time, and volunteered to make the cross-stitch kneelers and cushions in the Prisoner's Pew in St Peter's Church when the refurbishment of the pews began in 1978. They ran the 999 service after the automation of the telephone exchange in 1979, because they were the only place on Sark manned for 24 hours a day. Sark misses the Trinity House men.

The last visit to Point Robert lighthouse, seen here above the Bon Marin, *one of the Sark ferries.*

~

There were more goodbyes in November 1983. That was when the island said goodbye to the much loved cargo boat, the *Ile de Serk* and to Mr Henry Carré as harbourmaster. The Ile was built as a torpedo retriever at the end of the war, but never used as such. She came to Sark in 1947, the built-in derrick ideal for unloading the cargo, because although the island had two fixed cranes, they were both small, hand cranked ones. She was a splendid sea boat, her open deck above the bridge the ideal place for the trip from Guernsey to Sark. She carried everything! In November 1981 she took Richard Dewe's herd of Guernsey cows over to Guernsey when he gave up farming, when we had the delight of watching harbourmaster Henry Carré and skipper Peter Falla trying to push a recalcitrant cow into a horse box.

A dual farewell – Harbourmaster Henry Carré retired at the same time as the cargo boat the Ile de Serk. *He led the crew and islanders in a sea shanty, standing on the Ile's hatch cover.*

Sark being Sark, the farewell to the *Ile* was an excuse for a party. Henry Carré was presented with a tankard to mark his many years of service to the Isle of Sark Shipping Company, and there was a thank you cheque from the people of Sark for him as well. This all took place on the deck of the *Ile*, the party brought to a close by Henry singing a sea shanty. We stood on the Maseline quay and watched the lights of the *Ile de Serk* as she chugged away, saluted by a hoot from Point Robert, sad to think that Board of Trade regulations made it impossible for us to use her. However, as you will see, the *Ile* came back.

~

November is also tax month. Contrary to popular belief, Sark does have taxes although it does not have income tax. There is a Property Tax, known as *La Taxe*, and a wealth tax, based on visible wealth. In such a small community, people know how rich or poor people are, so there are no forms to fill in or bureaucracy to contend with. The tax rates are set by Chief Pleas on the advice of the Douzaine and collected by the Douzaine through the Constable. The Douzaine is the senior Chief Pleas committee, 12-strong, comprising both deputies and *tenants*. It is the administrative body of the island, overseeing island property and roads, employing the island workmen.

The taxes are collected by the Constable and the Vingtenier on the third Saturday in November, although it can be paid before then; the tax account is sent out after the Michaelmas Chief Pleas in October. *La Taxe* is used exclusively to help those in need.

Sark is not a welfare state; there is no old age pension here, nor unemployment benefit. If you don't work, you don't eat! There is no National Health here, either. The island has a private health insurance scheme, and La Taxe helps older residents to pay their premiums if they need help. The older members of the community live on the money they have saved during their lifetime, but if any disaster overtakes them, the island will help, using *La Taxe* to do so.

Until quite recently the Constables sat in the Senior School to collect the taxes, but now they can use the new committee rooms, opened by the Duchess of Gloucester in 1992. It is the only office block on Sark!

~

By the end of the month some of the holiday makers have returned, rehearsals for the Theatre Group productions are under way, the darts, snooker, pool, billiards and quiz competitions are beginning. Societies have regular meetings and winter life is well away. There was an active Film Society until the cost of hiring and showing 'Appointment with Venus', starring David Niven, Glynis Johns and Kenneth More and shot on Sark in the 1950s, rose so much that it no longer subsidised a winter programme. Then everyone bought videos, and we could have 'Appointment with Venus' and any other film whenever we wanted it at home. End of Film Society!

At the very end of the month the first taste of Christmas appears. On the last Sunday of November, or occasionally in early December, the Methodist Church holds its Toy Service. This is a splendid start to a self-indulgent season. Sark children look out good toys and take them to the service to give them to the British Red Cross for distribution to children in distress, in hospital or just in need. The service is always early so that the toys reach their destination in time for Christmas. The service marks the end of autumn and the beginning of winter!

~

LES AUTELETS AND BRECQHOU FROM L'EPERQUERIE

DECEMBER

DECEMBER IS THE MONTH WHEN Sark is definitely in another time-zone. Dickens would not have felt too out of place on Sark at Christmas time. The Avenue is too small to take on the commercial aspect of most High Streets. There are Christmas goods in the shops and decorated windows with fairy lights, but it is on a human scale, on a par with Christmas trees in house windows, not with the glitz of the money-catchers backed by superstores. Christmas on Sark is still a family festival with church-going a definite part of the celebration.

~

However, that is all later in the month. Other things do take place in December. It is the month in which Deputies of the People are elected. Sark, with its own small parliament, could have 52 members of parliament to represent its 560 inhabitants. The 40 *tenants* each have a seat, and since 1922 there are 12 elected deputies of the people.

These serve for three years and are eligible for re-election at the end of their term of office. There are usually more candidates than seats and the residents of a year and a day or more go to the polls to choose their deputies on a Tuesday at the beginning of December.

The polls are open from noon until 8pm and the counting, which is done by the Douzaine, is usually completed by 10pm.

The deputies take an oath in the Seneschal's Court swearing to do such duties as are asked of them until their term of office is over. Needless to say, no one is paid. It is a service to the community, not a career. If, at the end of their three years, they decide it is too much for them, they can stand down and carry on with their work.

~

Living on a small island does have its drawbacks when it comes to shopping. We all know what is in the shops, how much it costs and even how many there are! So a lot of Christmas shopping has to come from the more anonymous Guernsey. That means careful planning. At present there are two shopping trips a week on Wednesdays and Saturdays, so when everyone else is saying 20 or 30 more shopping days to Christmas, we are saying six or eight more shopping trips to Christmas.

The Ile de Serk *in a well-remembered role – decorated with a Christmas tree, ready for a Christmas shopping trip to Guernsey.*

It was even more difficult in the past when there was one weekday trip a week and one Saturday trip a month. In those days there was always a special Christmas Shopping Trip on a Saturday in the old Ile de Serk, decorated with a Christmas tree at her mast head, with a bar on board for the occasion. The men made a day out of it, supposedly for shopping, but actually a day out with the boys!

There would be a large Sark contingent lunching in the St Peter Port hotel nearest to the Sark berth at the White Rock and every second person in the High Street was from Sark. People would aim to come home on the Christmas shopping trip and the end of the White Rock quay in St Peter Port harbour would be knee-deep in suitcases and shopping bags and very merry people. The scene at the Sark harbour as the trip arrived was amazing. On one particularly rough day when the boat unloaded through the stone steps in the Creux Harbour mouth, one gentleman was passed shoulder-high up to the quay without realising that he had come ashore! It was more fun, if less convenient, than the present, more frequent, trips.

~

The school begins the Christmas feeling with its Christmas Fayre. The children work hard, making crackers, pot-holders, pencil-holders, decorative candle arrangements, calendars and other appropriate handicrafted artefacts. Mothers supply home-made preserves, cakes and scones. The sale starts at 2.00pm on a Friday afternoon, and by 2.30 the stalls are almost bare. The childrens' crackers are well-made and much sought after; so much so that the rule is parents only until 2.30, then any unsold go to the first buyer. The profit from the sale goes to the School Fund, which helps to finance any out-of-school activities. Fund raising plays a large part in the seasonal events!

Sark is too small to have a flower shop, and flowers are an essential part of Christmas. There is a chance to buy cut flowers and potted plants at another charity event, the Christmas lunch and sale at the Island Hall. This takes place in the week before Christmas and jumble, books, home-made preserves and cakes, local cream and butter join the plant stall, the opening after a full Christmas dinner, complete with crackers and presents for everyone. The plants go like hot cakes, a queue forming outside the Hall door as eager shoppers take the chance of getting popular Christmas presents without leaving the island.

The men start returning from their work on the Christmas trees as the month progresses. They come back in ones and twos as their particular tasks end, and the Christmas trees appear in the homes as they come on to the island with the men. In the past many of them returned on the Christmas shopping trip, adding to the general holiday air of the day.

The next happening is the Schools' Carol Service. This varies with the teachers. In the past the children had a traditional service of nine lessons and carols, the lessons not necessarily the usual ones. The James II Bible was used, the children working hard to understand and read the archaic English, and doing a good job of it. St Peter's Church is undecorated during Advent, but the Christmas tree presented to the church by the Company that employs the Sark men always makes sure that a beautiful tree arrives in time for the schools' service. It is put up and decorated on the Monday of the last week of term, the carol service always being on the last Tuesday.

In this community, everyone either knows or is related to a schoolchild, and the church is full to hear the service. In recent years the traditional form has given way to a more informal celebration, with poems and modern carols and songs following the Christmas story, giving variety to the services.

The schools' service is always on the same day so that it fits in with the carol singing that takes place in the same week. That is another fund-raising excercise, but it is also great fun and very much part of a traditional Sark Christmas. There are no small disorganised groups turning up on a doorstep, singing one verse and tapping the door here. Carol singing is organised. Anyone can join in, but there is only one group, and that group divides the island into five sections and advertises in advance which route will be followed on a particular evening. The houses on that route may pay the singers to stay away, if they have illness, a new baby or an excitable pet to be disturbed, but everyone else gets a visit.

Some of the houses on each route invite the carol singers in for refreshments; sausage rolls, mince pies, hot chocolate, mulled wine and home-made biscuits are among the offerings. Other houses provide sweets to moisten dry throats and almost everyone comes to a door or window to join in. Children are kept up or wakened to hear the carols. The group are usually warmly dressed and sing by the light of a lantern hung on a pole held up by a sturdy man. Except for the modern ski suits and anoraks, the picture is pure Victorian, the quartz crystals in the old granite walls of the buildings glittering in the lantern glow, the faces timeless and, with any luck, the whole thing under a clear sky with the winter starlight bright enough to see by.

The carol singers visit every house to sing, collecting for local charities.

That's with luck. It takes a lot to deter the carol singers, and they may sing with cold rain trickling down their necks, squelching boots and wet gloves. On a couple of memorable nights they have sung with snow flakes drifting across the lantern light, whitening their shoulders and adding a special magic to the scene. No one minded the cold or the wet on those nights.

The most beautiful route is the southern one, which crosses La Coupée to Little Sark. Then the added beauty of a navy-blue sea with Guernsey lights glinting across the water and a silver moonpath breaking into myriad sparkles in Grande Grève – the Plough, Orion and Sirius and Taurus with the Pleiades circling the North Star in brilliant formation overhead all make the long trek well worthwhile. Little Sark hospitality, traditionally enhanced by pea soup, home-cured ham and sausage pie, lures those with more mundane interests to join the southern route!

The school has a party to round off the year; term ends and the next excitement is a visit from Father Christmas. Sometimes he arrives on a boat, sometimes he appears with a pony and sled from somewhere at the north of the island, but, beard, tunic, boots and all, he meets the children in The Avenue, either by the Post Office or at La Collinette. He always has a large sack with him, and, surrounded by very excited children, he walks along the Avenue, sending parcels in to shopkeepers as he goes, helped by the children.

In the past the Royal Antediluvian Order of Buffaloes arranged a party for the children in the Mermaid, their headquarters, where Father Christmas gave presents to every child of school age on the island. More recently the party has moved to the Island Hall, where there is more space and games are organised, with a tea. Christmas festivities have begun!

The Buffs arrange another Christmas treat these days, a lunch for the older members of the community at Le Fleur du Jardin, a second chance in the year for old friends to meet and exchange news. In 1993 yet another treat arrived in the shape of the Salvation Army Band. They played carols in The Avenue, and travelled round the island by horse and carriage to play to all the housebound. Bands are very popular with Sark residents, and that was a splendid surprise. The band is hoping to do it again!

By this time Christmas goodwill is in full flight. There are two carol services, the traditional nine lessons and carols at St Peter's Church and a candlelit evening service at the Methodist Church. St Peter's Church choir sings at both. The island is very ecumenical, each church supporting the other.

The annual visit from Father Christmas blocks up The Avenue.

The morning service takes place in a church still bare for Advent, except for the Christmas tree, but the beauty of the familiar words and tunes makes it a warm, enjoyable service. The Methodist Church is bathed in golden candlelight, the windows dark and the lights of Guernsey just visible across the sea. It is a more informal service, often with Christmas poems included in the readings. Afterwards the congregation is invited to tea in the Methodist Schoolroom, with another chance to chat, so rare in the summer, so much enjoyed in the winter. Then the choir wraps up its robes – it is usually windy and rainy! – and gets them back to St Peter's Church for the next service.

That is usually on Christmas Eve. Before that the church is transformed from its sober white-washed normality into a welcoming bower of green, red and gold. An army of helpers lay fir branches on the window sills, tie them round the pulpit and along the lamp standards. A beautiful candle spiral rises above the altar, surrounded by greenery, poinsettas and gilded cones. Flower arrangements in glowing reds, bronzes and whites stand by the altar, the organ, the lectern and on any other unoccupied flat surface. Candles form a centre piece on each window-sill. A lighted crib, a candle-powered carousel of the journeys to the stable and everything is ready for the celebration. The contrast between the cold outside air and the warm fir-scented, glinting interior adds to the welcoming atmosphere.

Christmas Eve has a distinct holiday air. When customers go into the Bakery for their Christmas bread, mince pies, sausage rolls and other Christmas goodies they are likely to be served by pantomime characters, people from fairy stories or some other theme. There were Christmas puddings, turkeys, Christmas fairies and trees one year. The latest was Snow White and the Seven Dwarves, with Dopey slicing up your loaf for you and Grumpy finding the elusive icing sugar. Other shops have drinks and nibbles for all their customers. It is possible to have a very convivial lunch moving from the Gallery Stores to the Perfumery!

The shops shut at 5.30 and the first Christmas Service starts officially at the same time, but actually just a little later to allow people time to get there from the shops. The congregation are given unlit candles as they enter. The children's Candle Service is one of the most popular of them all. Families come en masse, the pews are lively with young voices, but not only the families. The church is crowded, which means that well over a quarter of the population is in church.

The service is short and simple; a carol, then total darkness as the vicar explains how light came to the world. A single candle comes down the church from the back, the flame flickering, and it lights the altar candles. Two young choristers light hand candles from the altar, then move back through the church, lighting the candles at the end

of the rows. The flame is passed along the pew from candle to candle. As the choristers move back, the light grows and the childrens' rapt faces are revealed. A familiar carol which does not need to be read is sung and, when all the candles are alight, the children process round the church and approach the crib, to see the Christmas story represented before the lights come up and the candles are dowsed. Another carol, and the service is over, the children taking the idea of Christmas away with them before they are swamped by presents.

Parents have the last-minute panic of wrapping and hiding, of calming down and bedding, of food preparation and pre-cooking. There is one hotel that stays open over the holiday, but most Sark people eat with family or friends. Any single person will be invited into a household; if anyone does spend Christmas Day alone, it is from choice! Most Christmas lunches are eaten in groups of at least ten.

The younger folk repair to the pubs for the evening, where there may be a band or a folk group or just convivial company. There are extensions at both the Mermaid and the Bel Air, but the crowd thins out at 11.30 as people go to the Midnight Eucharist. Sark still uses the older form of service, which visitors have to dredge up from their childhood. The triumphant 'Yea, Lord, we greet Thee, born this hap-py morning' rings through the church and Christmas has come. Afterwards people gather under the light outside the porch and exchange greetings and kisses before some nip back to the pub for a final drink, some go to friends for their first visit of the day and some rush back home to complete their tasks for later.

Christmas Day has shooting matches in the morning to get the men out of the house while the meal is finished and the children play with their stocking presents. The ones under the treee are distributed after lunch, when aunts, uncles, friends and guests call. Animals are exercised and fed, farm jobs done and everyone settles down to an evening of talk and cards, of silly games and sandwiches and a final retirement, soaked in peace and *bonhomie*.

Boxing Day shakes people out of the Christmas lethargy with another clay pipe shoot, a clay pigeon shoot and a fishing competition. There is often a mounted Treasure Hunt after Christmas too, to provide entertainment for younger people. The fishing competition is great fun, not only for the fishermen (and women and children) but for everyone at the weigh-in and auction at the Mermaid in the afternoon. The smaller boats go back into the water for the day and if the weather is kind there is a good supply of fresh fish for local freezers.

The weigh-in is in the late afternoon and the prizes for shore and boat catches are presented before the auction. Then fishermen will cheerfully bid for fish they have spent all day catching, the prices rising for a fine pollack, a bass or even a turbot. In a bad year, when the weather keeps the boats ashore and makes fishing off the rocks hazardous, other things are auctioned. It wasn't so long ago that a lad who is now a *tenant* and a sober member of Chief Pleas was fitted out with a tail and auctioned as a mermaid! He was quite a fund-raiser too. 'Jaws' appeared on another occasion. Bad weather does not stop the auction!

The 1993 Boxing Day auction raised £911 for the RNLI. Add this to the £674 raised by the carol singers, the £670 from the charity lunch and the £500-plus made by the children, and you have some idea of what happens during a Christmas season in Sark. It is a season of giving.

~

The week between Christmas and New Year is still family time, with those who have to return to the mainland anxiously watching the weather and the boats to make sure that they catch the connections. There are parties on New Year's Eve in the pubs and in private houses, with the old year rung out on St Peter's church bell, sometimes with an organ accompaniment. The bell rings out over quiet fields and houses, often under a starry sky or in bright moonlight. There is a pause before midnight, to give the clock a chance to strike – it strikes on the bell – which gives you time to raise a glass to toast present and absent friends and to wish the old year, and December, farewell.

~

THE SENIOR SCHOOL
AND CHIEF PLEAS' COMMITTEE ROOMS

JANUARY

AFTER THE SOUND OF THE bell dies away in the night air, there is a general kissing of family and friends and the new year starts in a flurry of good wishes. Some parties finish with breakfast, but that doesn't mean a late start to New Year's Day. New Year's Day is another holiday, marked by some daft happening to raise money for a charity besides the usual shooting competitions. Shooting and fishing are popular in Sark because you do not need a large team for a competition. The small population makes it impossible to get two teams in the winter to compete against each other seriously. So any games are strictly for fun, with mixed teams encompassing all ages.

The happenings really are daft, too! In past years people have turned out to watch a Boat Race – coxed fours rowing along the roads of Sark. We haven't got a river, the sea is far too rough to use at this time of year, so Oxford and Cambridge took to the roads. The home-made shells were allowed wheels underneath them, but had to use the oars to move themselves! They raced across the width of the island, along the Rue Lucas and down the hill to the Bel Air, the finishing line. They ended in a rush, but progress along the flat was a bit slow and painful!

New Year's Day and Oxford and Cambridge race along the roads.

Another year, another stunt, this time Roman chariot races with slaves in the shafts instead of horses. The costumes were impressive; helmets, shields and swords of the right period – in some cases. Others took a few liberties with Roman dress. An amazing number of the slaves were dressed as senators! The race was quite straightforward until the Fire Brigade decided that the competitors needed to be cooled down, after which there was an intermittent and unpredictable spray of water to add to the hazards.

There have been fancy dress hockey matches (no one on Sark plays serious hockey), bicycle polo, man-powered Grand Prix, boules matches (people do play boules, so that was dangerously sensible) but the best of all wasn't actually held on New Year's Day, but a bit before. If Christmas and New Year's Day fall on a Sunday, there is no relaxation of Sunday laws. The pubs cannot open and tractors can only be used for essential agricultural work. Daft happenings are displaced to other days to allow for a celebratory drink afterwards! So the ascent of the north face of the Bel Air was not actually on New Year's Day.

Climbing the north face of the Bel Air – a displaced New Year's Day frolic.

The climb was a hard one. Two climbers, assisted by two shirkers (yes, shirkers!) and harried by an abominable snowman, tackled the length of road from the top of the harbour hill, via Gas Bottle Ridge, to the summit at the Harbour bar in Bel Air. They climbed horizontally, of course, but they treated it as if it were vertical, searching for rocks in the road to use as handholds, roped together, finding anchor-age for the ropes and setting up a camp by what is now the Tourist Information Office. The exploit was all videoed at right angles – it looked most impressive on screen until a dog ran across the picture from bottom to top! It was hilarious, and raised £160 for local charities.

So the year always gets off to a lively start, to end the holiday with a flourish. Christmas is the only public holiday that Sark enjoys with the rest of the world! All the other bank holidays are spent catering for the needs of the hundreds of holiday makers who come to Sark for the day. The only other time that Sark has time off is when the island is closed. The island closed down for the celebration of the Queen's Silver Jubilee, for the wedding of the Prince and Princess of Wales, and it is closed for Royal visits. Otherwise it is business as usual except for Christmas and the New Year, which is why these holidays are so much enjoyed.

~

With the holiday over, Sark settles down to the winter work again. The hotels do all their repairs and redecoration, usually beginning in January. They may keep one member of staff to deal with enquiries or reservations, but it is frequently a local girl who helps out. The redecorating is done with local labour, along with any major changes to the hotels. The island itself gets on with major building projects while the roads are still clear of horses and visitors.

Today the line of horses and carriages waiting at the top of the harbour hill in the lay-by are a familiar sight, but that is fairly recent. The lay-by was completed in January 1982. Before that, we had real traffic jams in high summer at the top of the harbour hill.

The horses and carriages lined up from the gable end of the Bel Air up the hill to the crossroads, along both roads past the two banks and anywhere else they could find. The queues stretched down the hill on the way to Les Lâches as drivers waited for their passengers to come up the hill from the boats. On a cargo day, tractors were moving up and down with loaded or empty trailers and, as the carriages nearest to Bel Air filled up and moved off, other carriages drove down to take their places. It got to the stage of an accident waiting to happen. If one of the horses had been stung by an insect and had bolted....

The Douzaine decided to do something about it before that happened. The tenant who owned the land adjacent to La Collinette crossroads was approached, and was happy to donate a strip of land to the island. The digging began and a retaining wall was built and by January 1982 the lay-by was ready. It certainly improved the situation; the horses have stood happily facing the road ever since. Today many more of the carriage rides are pre-booked, so that the driver does not have to arrive early in the morning to make sure of a place near the harbour hill transport stop. The carriages are in position before the scheduled arrival time of the boat and can leave fairly quickly. That too has helped to ease the jams. Of course, when the boats are late for some reason, problems can arise, but not on the scale of the pre-lay-by days.

Horses and carriages waiting in the lay-by at the top of the harbour hill.

Before that, of course, the carriages went right down to the quays for their passengers. Those days were more leisurely. The visiting boats were larger and fewer and visitors spent an entire day on Sark. Pre-arranged tours were unknown. Then the pattern changed. More, smaller boats visit the island and since the mid 1970s many of the visitors come on tours, with a pre-booked carriage ride. The time they spend on Sark is less. The horses no longer go down harbour hill because it takes much longer, and passengers would have to walk up the steepest part. Today the toastracks bring passengers up the hill. Only members of the Royal family ride up the hill behind a horse in modern times! Most people get into their carriages in the lay-by.

~

January is Chief Pleas month again. The Christmas meeting of Chief Pleas takes place on the third Wednesday in January. These days it is the meeting at which the estimated Budget is presented to the house. Since 1983 Sark's financial year runs from January to December.

The budget is managed by Sark's Treasurer, the island's income coming from the impôt or tax on tobacco, wines and spirits, from the poll tax which is a part of every boat ticket to the island and from other sources. From its small income Sark pays its employees, such as the island workmen, the teachers, and the officers of the court. The Constable and Vingtenier, the island's policemen, are unpaid, but each serve for only two years.

Apart from wages, the island has to pay for the maintenance of the harbours and roads, the maintenance of the teachers' houses and medical centre and for the island's education.

Sark actually pioneered free, compulsory education. The Boys School, where Chief Pleas meets, was built in 1826, and that was when the law stating that each child on Sark must be educated was passed. Sark provides three schools now, for infants, from 5 to 7, for juniors, from 7 to 9 and for seniors, from 9 to 16. There is a teacher for each school and usually about 35 children in all three schools. The children cannot take qualifying examinations on Sark, but they can sit an 11-plus exam and if they pass that the island will pay for them to be educated off Sark. What they get if they remain on Sark is a truly individual education. The teacher/pupil ratio is very low!

When the island's expenditure is balanced with its income, Chief Pleas can get on with the rest of its agenda, deciding on problems of housing, of road traffic, of the demands of the modern world in the shape of measures for controlling drugs and generally ensuring that Sark can survive in a rapidly changing society. As an associate of the EEC, Chief Pleas had to give permission for Greece to join the Community, discussing the matter on the same agenda as a decision to make the Avenue one way. The few visitors who see a meeting of Chief Pleas are fascinated by the curious combination of international and parochial matters.

~

Meanwhile, outside, the natural world carries on. Halfway through the month the green spears of daffodils appear, and there are blossoms in sheltered valleys by the end of the month. The camellias began blooming at Christmas, and are in full flower in January. Very rarely, we have snow in January, but it usually comes later in the year – if we get it at all!

If it is not too wet, the farmers get on with their ploughing and planting. Dairy farming has shrunk in recent years. Two farms supply the island with milk, one which delivers daily and one which supplies the Island stores. Other farms just have cows for their own use. Sark's rich, creamy milk is not as popular as it used to be, and both dairy farms separate milk and cream to supply skimmed milk. The extra cream is made into butter or ice-cream, both of which are local treats. At this time of year, the extra cream is churned into butter which is frozen for use in the summer months, when hotels need milk and cream.

The hotels take a lot of the locally produced vegetables, too. Fresh salad plants, cauliflower, cabbage and broccoli are in demand. The local market gardeners produce a lot of the island's potatoes, too. Some come from farms, but gardens and plots produce quite a bit! The ground is dug over and prepared now if the weather is suitable.

January is often a fairly wet, windy month, however. The wells come up after a winter's rain. There is no central water supply on Sark. Each household has to supply its own water, from wells or boreholes or from catchment. Some houses have large underground tanks to store the winter rainfall for summer use. La Société Serquiaise has been measuring the rise and fall of the water table on Sark since 1976. It discovered that there was not one water table, spread evenly over the plateau, but a patchwork of independent water tables. Wells within ten feet of each other behave quite differently, rising and falling on a different time scale. All of them, however, reach a peak at the beginning of the year, then sink slowly through the season. Local people are very sparing of water, but visitors, accustomed to resevoirs and piped water, use it prodigally.

We are much closer to the problems of living, having to supply our own water, dispose of our own sewage and sort our own rubbish. Paper, tins and some bottles are recycled here, although we have to pay for some of it. Batteries are collected and exported, everything that can be composted is composted and we only burn if there is no alternative. Unfortunately it costs quite a bit to export some items, but the Environmental Group does its best to keep recycling viable.

The early months of the year are often saddened by a funeral as the older members of the community succumb to cold and damp, not to mention short, dreary days. This is a very small community and we all know one another. A death affects everyone. Today there are very few true Sark funerals, with the coffin carried by a team of bearers from the house to the church with the mourners following. More people die in hospital in Guernsey and the coffin is brought back to spend the night in St Peter's Church be-fore the service, This is usually on a Wednesday or a Friday, when the boats come in the morning and leave in the afternoon and friends and family from the other islands can get to Sark for the day. The service is about noon, to allow those who are at work to attend.

Even when someone dies on the island, the pattern has changed. The coffin is kept at home until the day before the funeral, then taken to church for the night. People do not want to subject their families to a long, sad walk and ask not to have a traditional funeral. There are still bearers, who are recruited from more distant family and friends, to carry the coffin from the church to the cemetery, a last service to the dead. Any death affects the island, which is quiet for some days after a funeral.

For the rest of the month, the winter competitions keep going, the Theatre Group carries on with its rehearsals, the fishermen scrape and paint their boats, strip and clean their engines and another batch of people go off on holiday somewhere.

~

Island maintenance continues. In 1982, there was a major overhaul of the church bell tower. The bell supports and the louvres were replaced. The removal of the old louvres made it possible to see the bell more clearly and to get a wonderful panoramic view of the island. When the tower was built, the Seigneur, W T Collings, went to the top and drew a panoramic view from there. In 1982, the Seigneur Mr Michael Beaumont took his camera up there and did the same thing. Parts of the island look the same, but the trees and many of the buildings show a lot of changes.

The bell itself is interesting. There is an inscription on it. It reads:

A D 1883
FONDUE AUX FRAIS DE QUELQUES AMIS
DE DEUX CANONS DON DU GOUVERNEMENT
A L'EGLISE DE SERCQ
W.F. COLLINGS. SEIGNEUR
G. VERMEIL, M. NISTRE

VENEZ MONTONS A LA MAISON DE L'ETERNEL

That says:

CAST AT THE EXPENSE OF SOME FRIENDS
FROM TWO CANNONS GIVEN BY THE GOVERNMENT
TO THE SARK CHURCH

So the St Peter's Church bell was once a couple of guns!

~

THE PILCHER MONUMENT

FEBRUARY

FEBRUARY MAY BE COLD AND grey, but it brings with it the first signs of spring. The daffodils are dancing yellow in the wind, just as if they were in a Wordsworth poem, and towards the end of the month the banks are starred with the bright yellow of the little celandines. If the year is mild the first primroses and violets appear as well. So there are enough signs that summer will come.

These signs are masked in some years. If we are going to have snow, it arrives in February, more often than not. Snow is rare, and it frequently comes on a south wind. We get snow when France does. The north wind crosses the Channel and warms up to bring us rain unless it is unusually cold. It's the north-easters, the easterlies and the southerly winds, blowing from across cold land, that results in snow in the Channel Islands.

When it does come, it is magical! Sark doesn't have traffic

Opposite: The Avenue in the snow.

problems. Tractors can get through almost anything – although in 1986, when there was very little snow but a prolonged, icy north-easter, the wind polished the harbour hill to glass and caused a few problems. We actually wished we had snow that year. The cold went on and on, killing the veronica bushes, damaging the tender plants, turning all the remaining leaves black as frosty day followed frosty day. That was the year in which we discovered that outside water tanks and unlagged pipes were no longer possible. There had not been a really cold winter within living memory before that, and no winter protection had been necessary. 1986 changed all that, pipes are all lagged now.

An unusual view of the Gallery Stores and Sark's single post box.

Snow does protect from that intense cold, and we had thick snow in 1985 and 1987. The sun came out to glisten on the uninterrupted white fields, roads and house tops. The daffodils bloomed gold above silvery-white gardens with blue shadows beside the trees. Children were let out of school to indulge in a snowman competition, the farmers hastily sought shelter for sheep and horses and carried hay to feed them. Cattle kept to their sheds, let out briefly to allow cleaning.

The animals actually fared better in the snow than they did in the long frost. The normally mild winters mean that many horses do not have stables. They usually spend all their time in the open. They quickly learnt to scrape the snow aside, but even with New Zealand rugs and plenty of hay they found the cold wind of 1986 a trial. They all survived, however!

Everyone enjoyed the snow. Men quickly made sleds, or resorted to trays to toboggan down slopes on Derrible common, the Eperquerie, Dos d'Ane and any other suitable slope. Age was no bar to a good snowball fight either.

Going down to sea level was amazing. The Maseline quay hand-rail was hung with fringes of icicles, the tunnel mouth decorated with curved teeth all made of ice. The Creux Harbour was a foot deep in snow, the fishing boats all cloaked in white. The beach was white, with a sharp demarcation line at high-water mark. The cliffs had snow caught in cracks and ledges, criss-crossing the rock face with white lines. The sea had frozen, glassy green at the foot of the cliffs. With the sun out, the white plateau and white shaded cliffs were set off by the the blue sky and darker blue sea, all sparkling bright.

Ashore, La Coupée looked amazing, blocked at the ends between its high banks by drifting snow. The road had to be dug out to allow the tractors from Little Sark through. At the island's highest point, the pink-washed Mill Cottage glowed on its hill top against the surrounding white. As the snow was compacted and turned into ice by tractors, cycling became more difficult, particularly when overnight frost made the tracks even more slippery. Island workmen collected salty sand from the Creux Harbour at low tide to scatter on the roads, and the snow and ice slowly vanished to leave brown roads through the white hedges.

The Sark visitors hardly ever see. The Maseline Harbour with ice-coated railings and bollards.

The snow doesn't last long. All too soon the fields are green and soggy, the banks brown again and the spring flowers open up to the light as they are uncovered. The cold doesn't stop the ormerers either. As soon as there is a low tide, whatever the weather, intrepid souls wade into icy seas and turn over rocks to find the elusive ormer.

~

Ormers are single shelled shellfish that browse on the algae covering rocks below tide level. They have very pretty shells with a row of holes along the side. They are not found across the channel, the Channel Islands are their northern limit. They are related to the American abalone and the New Zealand pau, and they are delicious! So delicious that they are protected. They may only be collected at the low spring tides at the equinoxes, and no artificial aids can be used – apart from the ormering hook, that is. So on ormering tides people put on old clothes, pick up the curved iron hooks for turning rocks and levering tightly clamped shells from their surfaces, and go down to the sea. Bold ormerers wade out and search thigh deep in cold seas; less hardy souls stick to the rarely exposed low tide mark. They don't find as many ormers, but they stay dry!

In the past ormers were collected by the tin bath load, but only the experts can fill a bucket today, although numbers are increasing now that they are protected from divers. They have to be cleaned and beaten, and can then be fried or casseroled. They can also be pickled, to provide a treat in the months without an ormering tide. Once this holiday period is over, February gets back to normal.

~

Normal for the farmers means lambs. Lambing may start as early as December, there have been both Christmas lambs and Christmas calves in recent years, and lambing goes on through January. By February there are pretty little animals frisking about the ewes, and often a few orphans or rejected twins in the farm kitchens. These hand-reared lambs are enchantingly tame. As far as they are concerned, humans mean food, and they will bound clumsily up to visitors, butting against their knees. Pam de Carteret's lambs actually go for walks with her and her dogs, following happily right round the island. They probably think that they are dogs!

Unhappily, the hand-reared lambs are not always integrated back into the flock, and may end up as meat – as most of their contemporaries on the cliffs will, too. Sark hotels usually serve local lamb and local pork. It is easy to tell the difference between imported meat and local meat – the local meat has more flavour.

It isn't always snowy in February. In 1983 the BBC came to Sark to do some filming for breakfast television, which was just beginning. They rode round a sunny island in a horse and carriage, but it was just as well that the temperature wasn't transmitted with the pictures. It was freezing! Still, the flowers were about and the sea looked lovely; even if warm underwear is needed, Sark is still beautiful.

Sark is part of the Bailiwick of Guernsey, along with Alderney. The Queen is represented in all three islands by the Lieutenant Governor of Guernsey, who often crosses to the two smaller islands for a visit. Sark is just a short boat ride from Guernsey, where His Excellency lives in Government House, and is ideal for an informal weekend break. The Lieutenant Governor and his lady often pop across to stay in the Seigneurie. Each Governor serves for about five years, as does the Lieutenant Governor of Jersey, and once in their tours of duty, both visit Sark on a joint courtesy visit. This often happens in February, before islanders are too busy to talk to the two Queen's representatives.

The two Lieutenant Governors, like most official visitors to Sark, visited the schools and talked to the children. The walls of all three schools are covered with their work – needlework, paintings, scrap books and handicrafts. One of their most impressive projects was far too big to be moved far, let alone put up on a wall. All the children raised funds for, and the boys actually made a mount for the cannon above the Banquettes landing at the north of the island.

During 1983 the children got permission to mount the cannon from the Seigneur, who owns it – and all the other cannon on Sark – and from tenant Dennis Hurden, as the cannon is on his côtils. They also researched the type of cannon, copying its markings and sending them to Portsmouth for identification. Then the whole school set about fundraising. They were helped by d'Hautrée school, in Jersey, help most gratefully accepted. The seasoned oak cost them £300 and it took another £150 to get it to Sark!

Work began in February 1984, when the children cleared the brambles from round the cannon, helped by Mr Tom Long, who was teaching them woodwork. Lawrence Roberts and his JCB were used to lift the cannon away from the cliff top into the field alongside his workshop and boatshed, where it was put on to blocks and cleaned. It took them a year and a half to complete the project. Boys who had to stand on boxes to reach the work bench when they started had grown a couple of feet or so by the time they finished. The cannon still stands on the concrete platform made for it above the Banquettes.

With such an example from the children, La Société Serquiaise funded more cannon mounts, and all but two are off the ground today.

All through February the many competitions in the pubs are moving through their heats towards the quarter finals. It is a good month to clear the games, and weekends are busy as darts and other contests are played off and quizzes go through their games. Finding a free evening is difficult! On a busy Saturday night in February 1990, well after 10pm, when everyone was enjoying themselves, testing their skills, the fire sirens wailed to herald one of the worst fires for many years.

~

There was a quiz night at the Bel Air, a darts match somewhere else and all the Seigneurie staff were out to dinner with the Seigneur and Mrs Beaumont, so that there was no one about at the Seigneurie. There had been a storm shortly before, which brought down the overhead power cables, and the Seigneurie farm had been using its back-up generator. The fire started by the cattle shed at the farm, and no one was in the vicinity to see the flames. By the time Mr John Jackson saw them from his kitchen and raised the alarm, the fire had a good hold. The sirens summoned firemen from dinner parties, from the quiz and from other revelries, most of them dressed in their best clothes. No one had a tractor out as it was after 10pm, when tractors must be off the road. The men rushed off to the fire station on borrowed bikes to find out where the fire was. Not that it was diffi-cult; the flames could be seen from St Peter's church.

At that stage the volunteer fire-fighters had no special protective clothing and their old-fashioned fire helmets were so heavy that they were an encumbrance. The mens' good clothes and shoes were ruined! The hoses had seen better days and leaked and there was no modern equipment. Even so the firemen slowly brought the blaze under control, and it was out by the early hours of Sunday morning.

The milking herd and the ponies were released and saved, but the two bulls and seven heifers died from the fumes before the fire-fighters reached the fire. When the site was inspected on Sunday, it appeared that the generator had started it. The island's community spirit was very apparent on that Sunday. Plenty of people turned up to clear up, and farmers brought offers of hay and feed for the remaining cows.

This all happened just after Trevor Kendall took over as fire chief. He was a fully trained fireman and had just begun a training programme for the volunteer fire-fighters. The fire helped to accelerate the modernisation of the Sark Fire Brigade.

Sark had no fire brigade until 1957. In that year the Pavilion, a pub at the Vauroque, burnt down in June and then Stock's Hotel annexe burnt down in November, with the loss of a life. Mr Freddy Hawkins organised the volunteer fire-fighters, who made their own wheeled water-tanks which could be hitched to a tractor. The telephone exchange was manual and manned for 24 hours a day, so the operators summoned firemen, who could get to a blaze anywhere on the island in five minutes.

That didn't help the next serious fire, in November 1969; Miss Margeurite Topliss died when her house caught fire. The house was back from the road, on a cliff-top, and was well ablaze by the time it was seen.

The Seigneurie farm fire highlighted the need for better equipment, and with a fireman with 32 years service in England taking over in 1990, everything was overhauled and updated. The tractor-drawn tanks are still the best way of getting water to a fire, but today they can be filled from swimming pools and underground tanks near to a fire. There are new hoses with high-powered pumps to back them up and the men are now trained in the use of breathing apparatus. They have proper protective clothing, boots and hats – no more spoiled suits!

All this expertise was needed in February 1993 when Plaisance, the house on the hill above La Coupée, caught fire. The flames were curling up out of the windows when the Fire Brigade got there, early in the morning, having been summoned by the owner who just managed to get himself and his wife down stairs and 'phoned for help before the fire damaged the stairs and burnt out the telephone. The Fire Brigade, with their new equipment and techniques, had the fire out within an hour, limiting the structural damage to the house by entering the smoke-filled kitchen with breathing apparatus to deal with the seat of the fire. A disaster averted!

~

There was another February disaster that could not be averted. On a windy Valentine's Day in 1990, part of the old twelfth century monastery wall in the Seigneurie grounds crashed down. Lumps of granite landed on the herb garden and bounced across the path exposing the earthen filling of the wall. The noise was deafening. The broken wall was a delayed victim of the 1987 hurricane. The wind funnelling up the Port du Moulin valley had uprooted many trees behind the wall, some of which fell across the top, damaging the capping stones.

Workmen sealing the old monastery wall in the Seigneurie grounds blended into the historical background!

With the trees gone, wind drove rain into the old wall and under the damaged stone capping, slowly washing the earthen filling away. Eventually a really strong wind finished the work, blowing down the top stones. It would have cost a small fortune to rebuild the top of the wall, so the rest of the dangerous stones were knocked down and the top sealed with concrete. The Seigneurie doves love it now, it makes an ideal morning basking site.

~

By the last days of February the end of the winter rest is in sight. The hotels begin their spring cleaning, using local help and people return from their holidays to finish the last tasks before the beginning of the season.

~

Les Autelets
off the north west coast

MARCH

SPRING HAS DEFINITELY ARRIVED IN March. The banks are thick with primroses and violets, the daffodils are dying down and the leaves are beginning to unfurl on the twigs overhead. The birds are going dotty, singing away to warn others off their territory, collecting dried grass, moss, lichen, horse hair and anything else likely to make a comfortable nest.

~

The variety of species is amazing. Wrens tucking their tiny bodies into even tinier crannies in walls, sparrows and chaffinches dropping grass from under the eaves of houses, blackbirds and thrushes hiding away in bushes, linnets, firecrests, warblers and robins taking over the trees. If you're lucky, you may see a tree creeper investigating likely niches behind the ivy stems. The swallows and house martins turn up and renovate old nests stuck on to walls or among the beams of barns and stables. The world is definitely waking up again.

Down at sea level the oyster catchers are back, and terns are investigating the isolated headlands for nesting sites. There are guillemots and razorbills quarrelling on the ledges on Les Autelets

117

and the fulmars are nesting around the Boutiques.

Mothering Sunday sends the children out into the fields to collect wild flowers to give to their mums during the Mothering Sunday service. This festival was not invented by greeting card manufacturers. Mothering Sunday dates from medieval times. It was the day on which apprentices were allowed a day off to visit their families. The apprentices worked long hours with very few holidays, but Mothering Sunday was one of them, and the apprentices would take a present for their mothers. The service is still observed on Sark, and children bring bunches of wild flowers that they have picked themselves to church, take them to the altar to be blessed and give them to their mothers.

The Women's World Day of Prayer is always observed on Sark, too. This international day of prayer has a service written by a different country every year. The various cultures are reflected in the choice of words and hymns, but no one religion predominates. In Sark the services alternate between the two churches and the participants are Anglican, Methodist, Roman Catholic and Buddhist, along with a few agnostics. The thought that the same service is rolling round the planet with the sun extends the sense of community from one small island to one planet.

The fishermen are down with their boats, which are still on the Creux Harbour quay, with most of the repainting finished and the engines back in place. They are finishing off the anti-fouling of the bottom of the boat, repainting their numbers and completing the annual overhaul of ropes and nets on the strings of lobster pots. The moorings are checked, the low spring tides making repairs to the chains and deadmen in the Creux Harbour easy. A diver is needed to inspect the moorings at Les Lâches and groups of fishermen join together to get the underwater chains and shackles checked and repaired.

The landlines are looked at and repaired before they take the strain of windblown fishing boats pulling at them in the southerly winds. Visiting boats often tie up to a fisherman's moorings while he is out at work, and cannot understand the irritation this causes.

Fishermen pay for their lines, to make sure that they are as secure as possible in summer storms. Sark has no safe harbour, the moorings are all the fishermen have to keep the boats that earn their living safe. The lines are geared to the weight of the owner's boat; heavier vessels will damage them, and so will two or more boats attached to the same mooring buoy. Hence the warning notices on the Creux Harbour sea wall and the annoyance of fishermen who come in to find a couple of power boats on their buoy.

The mobile crane is used to put boats into the water and take them out these days.

Not so long ago putting the boats into the water was a communal affair. Until 1983 the only cranes on the island were small, fixed, handcranked cranes. Only the one in the Maseline harbour was strong enough to launch the fishing boats, and the fishermen fixed a day in March when they all turned up and helped one another to wind their boats down into the sea. Heavy boats needed four men on the crane to control the rate of descent. There were a few beers to make the effort easier and everyone enjoyed the occasion. With such a communal effort needed to put boats into the water and to take them out again, it was not possible to take advantage of a period of calm weather to do a little wet fishing. Once the boats were out, they were out for the whole winter.

When Sark sold the *Ile de Serk*, with its derrick, it needed a larger crane to deal with the landing of the cargo. After some discussion, Chief Pleas decided that Sark should buy a mobile crane, small enough to go through the tunnels to both the Creux and Maseline quays and able to go up the hill and be used on the top of the island.

The mobile crane arrived in 1983. In March 1984 the old fixed cranes were to be moved to make more room on the quays. The crane in the Creux Harbour was moved quite easily, but the heavier one on the Maseline quay presented a problem. It was partially dismantled, and the arm removed by the mobile crane. As it tackled the next section, it overbalanced and the new crane, with a large part of the old crane, fell into the sea.

The crane driver was very lucky, in that it toppled slowly and he had time to get out of the cab and jump on to the quay. Everyone watched, appalled, as the crane disappeared under the water, blocking the access to the quay and leaving Sark with no cranes at all to unload cargo, even if the cargo boat could get alongside the quay. The crane was eventually lifted by flotation bags, and floated, just underwater, all the way to St Peter Port harbour, where there were cranes large enough to lift it ashore.

Luckily, the *Ile de Serk* had not been sold and was used again as cargo boat until the insurance was paid and Sark had a new crane. Equally luckily, one of the first jobs that the mobile crane had done was to assist in the strengthening of the piles in the Maseline jetty, so that the replacement mobile crane, when it arrived, was driven straight off the *Port Soif* on a high tide, straight on to the jetty, strong enough to bear it.

Not all the March work goes on at sea level. Up on the top of the island people are equally busy. The carriages are brought out, overhauled and repainted or varnished before they are tested and licensed for the road. The final refurbishment of rooms in hotels is nearing the end, and the various societies finish their winter programmes.

Before the mobile crane arrived, the fishermen banded together and lowered their boats by hand-cranking them. This was one of the boats lost in the 1987 Hurricane.

~

Sark is good at entertaining itself. The Sark Singers give at least one concert in a year. There are dancing classes, aerobics and other exercise sessions, recorder clubs and the Thursday Club, which has lunches and talks through the winter. In March the Theatre Group presents its annual production in the Island Hall, having rehearsed through the winter.

There is a long, strong theatrical tradition on the island. The present society has been going since 1962, and before that there were the SADS, the Sark Amateur Dramatic Society. The Theatre Group has tackled some ambitious productions in its career. It has produced musicals, farce, pantomime, thrillers, Victorian Music Hall, one act plays and Shakespeare. There is also the odd variety concert interspersed between the rest. Many people on Sark only ever see live theatre when the Theatre Group puts on its play, so the Group aims to stage something completely different every year, on the principle that every so often there will be something for everyone!

Sark has a problem in that it has no permanent stage, and that it is too expensive to hire the Hall every week for three months for rehearsals. Rehearsals take place in the Methodist schoolroom or in a restaurant. As these are rarely in use in the winter they make ideal rehearsal halls! The production doesn't transfer to the Island Hall un-til the week of the performance.

On a Saturday near the end of March, the stage manager begins his work. The flats are dragged out of their difficult storage places, the scenery is built and the stage is put up. Sometimes it is a conventional one, with a proscenium arch and curtains, sometimes it has a catwalk and for one memorable performance there were two stages, one at each end of the Hall.

That was for a farce that needed really solid scenery, so that doors could be slammed and windows climbed through. The set was far too sturdy to be struck in the first interval and rebuilt for the second act, then rebuilt again for the third act. In the absence of a revolving stage, Sark decided on a revolving audience. In the first interval everyone in the auditorium stood up, picked up their chairs, turned them round and faced the other way, to the second stage and a new set. In the second interval they reversed the process. Modern theatres go in for theatre in the round. Here we have audience in the round!

Once the stage is up, the electricians move in to set up the lights and any sound effects needed. They are still working on Sunday, with the set designer and decorators working round them. By Sunday evening the lights are working, the set is up and mostly painted and the curtains are hung. The chairs can be brought in.

A Sark Theatre Group production, an evening of Victorian entertainment!

Monday is technical rehearsal day, when the cast gets used to the entrances and exits and finds out if their costumes allow them to move where they are expected to move. Lighting cues and sound cues are rehearsed. Tuesday is usually dress rehearsal, with full make-up. If this is a total distaster then Wednesday is another! Amazingly, Wednesday is often a night off.

Thursday is the first night, and is usually about three-quarters-full. Sark audiences are generous and loyal. The Theatre Group is well supported. There are usually about a hundred seats in the Hall, and 560 people on Sark, including the babies and the immobile. The Group plays to good houses for three nights, with Friday and Saturday often a sell-out, with some people returning again.

The audiences are fairly predictable. Thursday is responsive, Friday is quiet but appreciative and Saturday is riotous, particularly if the production is a pantomime. There is no shortage of barrackers

– the audience participates with great enthusiasm. By the last night the cast is usually over its nerves; the actors feel as if they could do another week. On Saturday night, however, after the last performance, the electricians get to work and take down the lights, the make-up and wardrobe is packed up and a large part of the set dismantled.

There is a stage party, but not on the stage. Noble members offer their houses for unwinding in, presents are given to producer and stage manager and to other hardworking participants, such as piano players. The electricians and stage crew arrive late at the party, those with big parts leave fairly early, exhausted, and everyone turns up at the Hall on Sunday morning to finish clearing away. By Monday the Hall can be used for badminton, billiards, gym and all the other activities. You'd never know that it had been a theatre 36 hours before.

~

Once the play is over, we are definitely girding up our loins for the coming season. Even with imported help in the hotels, guest houses and stables, local people have to work long hours to accommodate the resident and the day visitors.

Most residents have more than one job, at least one of which is year-long. It isn't actually possible to make a living with one job, unless you're a hotel owner! Sark rates of pay are very low. A seasonal job won't keep anyone right through the winter. 'Ah, but you don't pay income tax' is the usual comment. True, but you do have to pay a monthly health insurance premium, La Taxe, electricity at 23p - 28p a unit and food with the cost of transport from Guernsey, the cost of electricity, the cost of the crane etc. all built into it. Lobsters and champagne may be relatively cheap, but just compare our meat and tea to mainland prices! You can't live on cigarettes and perfume.

So, with the leisurely winter holiday over, the busy season approaches. Tour companies are negotiating deals with carriage owners and and restaurateurs and looking for local couriers. Most day visitors come with tours these days, many with pre-booked meals and cycles or carriage rides. There are still intrepid explorers who arrive on the early boats and arrange everything for themselves, but many of them are Guernsey and Jersey residents having a day out. The freelance visitors certainly don't make up the bulk of the day visitors.

By the end of the month there are strangers to be seen in the Avenue. Good weather encourages the first visitors to come on the days when the boats come in the morning and return to Guernsey in the afternoon. After a winter surrounded by well-known faces, it is pleasant to see someone else. The style of life changes, adapting to one in which you don't know everyone.

Even though Sark has changed with the years, life here is still community life. The boundaries are extended by children at school off the island, holidays on the mainland or in other parts of the world. Work is made easier by tractors, cranes and other modern machinery, married youngsters want to live in their own houses instead of with their parents, but it is still a place where the air is fresh, where there is little danger of a mugging, where the family is important, granny can baby sit and the surroundings are beautiful. Life on Sark is good quality life!

~   ~   ~

The author as the Wicked Queen at a Sark Theatre Group party.
(Photograph courtesy Jane Cox)

About the author:

Jennifer Cochrane has lived on Sark since 1975, moving to the island from Central London. She is an author with some forty works published, writing children's ecology and natural history books, most of them found in schools. She also broadcasts on BBC Radio Guernsey and writes for the *Jersey Evening Post*. As she explains in this book, Sark residents have more than one job; another one of hers has been as a carriage driver, taking visitors on tours round Sark behind a horse, and she is still the secretary of the Sark Skilled Driving Society. She also works in the Seigneurie. An enthusiastic amateur actress, Jennifer Cochrane has produced plays and Music Hall and worked backstage in Sark Theatre Group Productions. She was elected as a Deputy of the People to Sark's parliament, Chief Pleas, at the end of 1993.

JERSEY RAMBLES: *Coast and Country*
by John Le Dain
127 pages; Pen & ink drawings & 28 maps; Price £4.95

Also available:

NO CAUSE FOR PANIC
Channel Islands Refugees, 1940-45
by Brian Ahier Read
159 pages; Fully illustrated; Price £6.95

SEAFLOWER BOOKS may be obtained through your local bookshop or direct from the publishers, post-free, on receipt of net price, at:

1 The Shambles
Bradford on Avon
Wiltshire
BA15 1JS

Tel/Fax 01225 863595

Please ask for a copy of our complete illustrated list of books.